Your
5-Minute
Personal
Coach

Valorie Burton

HARVEST HOUSE PUBLISHERS
EUGENE, OREGON

Cover by Koechel Peterson and Associates, Inc., Minneapolis, Minnesota

Cover photo by Jackie Hicks

Makeup artist: Kym Lee

Published in association with the literary agency of Alive Communications, Inc., 7680 Goddard Street, Ste #200, Colorado Springs, CO 80920.

YOUR 5-MINUTE PERSONAL COACH
Copyright © 2012 by Valorie Burton
Published by Harvest House Publishers
Eugene, Oregon 97402
www.harvesthousepublishers.com

ISBN 978-0-7369-3931-7 (pbk.)
ISBN 978-0-7369-4293-5 (eBook)

Printed in the United States of America

12 13 14 15 16 17 18 19 20 / VP-GLD / 10 9 8 7 6 5 4 3 2 1

Contents

Introduction

Over the years, I have had the wonderful privilege of writing to thousands of people each week, sharing what's on my heart and hoping it might inspire them with ideas and action steps to find greater fulfillment, joy, and resilience. My weekly e-newsletter, *The Coaching Session*, is my most basic way of expressing my purpose in life: inspiring others to live more fulfilling lives and using writing and speaking as a vehicle to do that.

The most thrilling part of this weekly journey is always the e-mails I receive in return: "How did you know I was dealing with that issue this week? These are just the words I needed!" Such comments always bring a smile to my face. They let me know that I've had the privilege of being used as a vessel, and that the seemingly random ideas that come to me to write about are not really so random at all. God's hand is always in it, even on a not-so-great writing day. My job is to get out of the way and let the words flow, trusting that they'll hold special meaning for you.

After more than a decade of this sort of writing, I've been asked to commit these weekly messages to book form. *Your 5-Minute Personal Coach* is the result! I've also packed this book with tools such as assessments, "Did You Know?" facts that you can apply to your life, and powerful coaching questions that will help you break through the barriers that hold you back from your true potential.

As a personal and executive coach and as the founder of an organization that trains professional coaches, it is my job to ask powerful questions. Over and over again, I have been amazed at the ability of the right question to unearth the answers that lay within us all along.

When you ask the right questions, you get the right answers.

But with the fast pace of life, we don't sit still long enough to ponder. We believe we are saving time by charging ahead with our plans, never pausing for a moment to be intentional about our next steps. I believe in the power of coaching to absolutely transform your life. In fact, it is part of my mission to help you learn to coach yourself. Coaching will, I hope, become a way of life for you. When faced with a dilemma, I want you to learn to pause and ask yourself the right question. Rather than panicking or worrying or soliciting everyone else's opinion (especially the opinions of those who are not wise or experienced enough to shed the light you need), I invite you instead to have a coaching moment. And this book is full of coaching moments.

I've packed each section with a coaching toolbox of 25 questions. Use these questions to get the powerful next steps that will propel your life forward. And use them with others! If you manage people or are a coach, parent, teacher, or lead people in any capacity, these questions can have a powerful impact.

Some coaching moments will be quick. As soon as you ask the question the answer will be so obvious that you won't need to journal about it or ponder it very long. In fact, you may find yourself saying, "Why didn't I ask myself that question in the first place?" For example, when you find yourself being unproductive or procrastinating, the simple question, "Is this how I really want to spend my time right now?" will likely yield a pointed answer: No. This will lead to the more important question: "So what am I going to shift my attention to right now?" It may sound elementary, but research actually confirms that the most successful, resilient people in life and in business are masters at coaching moments. These people are self-aware enough to notice their thoughts and intentionally change them to the ones that are the most productive and effective for achieving their goals—whether those goals are in relationships, work, finances, health, or your emotional or spiritual life.

Carry this book with you and pull it out when you have a spare moment. Put it next to the bed and read one of its messages first thing in the morning or in the evening before bedtime.

The messages within are tools to help you become more resilient and effective in every area of your life. You may choose to go through it one page at a time, applying the coaching questions to whichever dilemma or opportunity seems appropriate, or you may choose to skip ahead to the section of questions you think will be most helpful to you at the present time.

As you read through these pages, I hope you'll sense that I am writing to you as a friend, not an expert—as someone who wants to support you in moving your life to the next level, whatever that looks like for you. Over the years, I've received e-mails and notes from readers just like you who've read my coaching questions and had major breakthroughs—many of them begrudgingly. One woman wrote, "I'm so mad at you right now for asking those hard questions. I didn't want to answer them! But for some reason, I did anyway. I hate to admit it, but those tough questions were just what I needed."

Honesty isn't easy, and it takes courage to tell the truth. But the truth is the only answer that will move you forward authentically. If you don't tell yourself the truth, you can't possibly find real solutions that work. So as you read these pages, I want to encourage you to muster the courage to be honest. Give yourself permission not to know all the answers. Sometimes, the fact that you don't know the answer is all the answer you need for now. It is at those times that your job is to be patient and trust that the answer will come in God's divine timing. Simply admitting that you don't know allows you to take a breath and rest in that place of uncertainty. Perhaps that is the lesson for now.

I suggest you answer these questions either out loud or on paper. I've found that answering completely in your head is usually less effective. Because our thoughts tend to run on—one leads to another— you can make clearer connections and peel back the layers more easily if you articulate your thoughts either on paper or verbally. Having a trusted person to discuss your answers with or even talking out loud to yourself (hearing yourself say something aloud is a powerful tool!) are both effective ways to articulate your thoughts verbally. Using a journal or even typing your responses can be an effective way to articulate your thoughts in written form. Choose the method that works best for you. You might try different approaches and take note of which flows best. Of course, you don't always have someone available to talk to, so try at least one method that allows you to truly self-coach. In moments when you need to redirect your thoughts, perform on the spot, or get clear about your next step when no one else is around, you will have the skills and confidence to take the best course of action. I'm excited to join you on this journey!

Warmest wishes,

Valorie Burton

Part 1
Inner Resilience, Emotional and Spiritual Well-being

If you falter in a time of trouble,
how small is your strength!

PROVERBS 24:10

Did You Know?

Resilient people think differently. They have a
level of psychological capital and mental toughness
that enables better performance and
leadership under stress.

Think back to the achievement in your life you are most proud of. Whether it is the success of your marriage, your parenting skills, a career triumph, or the personal character you've developed through your own perseverance, your success could not have come about without one key trait: *Resilience*. Resilience is your ability to bounce back from setbacks, thrive, and grow in the face of adversity and change.

No matter what the goal, it is almost guaranteed there will be obstacles along the path to your vision. And the most successful people in the world are masters at bouncing back from setbacks. Whether the setback is small (such as an argument with your spouse or an unexpected expense that threw off your spending plan this month) or large (such as a layoff at work, cancer, or a divorce), your focus in life must continually be to recover from the unwanted detours so that you can stay on your path and enjoy victory.

Resilience is a skill, and we can all learn it and improve upon it. Sure, some people appear to bounce back effortlessly. There is a reason for that. They often have a certain combination of personal traits, resources, and skills that help them get back on their feet after suffering a disappointment. Researchers point out three elements that can empower an individual to be more resilient:

• Genetics

Some people are born with a more positive attitude that helps them deal with stress and adversity. Others have underlying mental health conditions that can be triggered under stress and undermine resilience. So whether for better or worse, your genes play a role in your resilience. However, the two other elements that contribute to your inner resilience are more within your control.

• Personal Resources

Personal resources include your friends, family, work environment, education, money, health, spiritual fortitude, previous experiences, and overall support system. When you encounter obstacles, your network of personal resources helps you surmount them.

• Thought Processes

Most important of all is how you *think* in the face of an obstacle. What you say to yourself in the face of adversity is the most significant predictor of how you will fare the storm. "For as he thinks in his heart, so is he," Proverbs 23:7 (NKJV) famously proclaims. It is absolutely true. What you think, you will become. Becoming more aware of your thoughts and being intentional about making them productive, positive, and truthful is essential to your success and well-being.

Your Resilience, Emotional, and Spiritual Health Checklist

Before you dive into this first section of the book, read these statements and check only the ones that are true for you *today*.

- [ ] I know my purpose and live it every day.

- [ ] I am not withholding forgiveness from anyone.

- [ ] Fear is not stopping me from moving forward on my most meaningful goals.

- [ ] I maintain a positive outlook most of the time.

- [ ] I have a strong support system of friends and family.

- [ ] I am spiritually mature and aware of God working in my life.

- [ ] I am in a good place emotionally. I am whole and well.

- [ ] My life is fulfilling and meaningful.

- [ ] I have a deep sense of joy and experience inner peace daily.

- [ ] In the last major challenge I faced, I was able to bounce back and move forward quickly.

- [ ] In a crisis, I usually remain calm and take action that is helpful to the situation.

- [ ] I can tolerate uncertainty without a high level of anxiety.

- [ ] Those who know me best would describe me as "adaptable to change."

☐ I am lighthearted and try to find humor even in difficult circumstances.

☐ I enjoy discovering new ways to do things.

☐ I am a good problem-solver.

☐ I always learn and find ways to apply the lessons from my past experiences.

☐ I am comfortable being myself.

☐ I am an empathetic listener.

☐ I have found purpose in my painful situations and believe all things work together for good.

___ Total

Rather than judging yourself if you cannot check off many of the statements, use this assessment as a tool to get clear about the items you want to be sure to check off in the future. You'll be working on making all of these statements a reality as you work through the coming pages. Make that your goal!

What is the most important question you need to answer in your life today?

*Go confidently in the direction of your dreams.
Live the life you have imagined.*

HENRY DAVID THOREAU

Point to Ponder:

*You can learn to coach yourself by taking moments to pause
and ask simple, thought-provoking questions that move you
in the right direction.*

One of the reasons so many people can't find the answers they need for the challenges they face is that they ask themselves the wrong questions—or never bother to ask questions at all. As a professional life coach, my primary job is to ask the right questions. I ask the kinds of questions that shift your perspective or help you see that the answer is obvious, even if the situation is complicated. One of the smartest things you can learn to do is coach yourself in the midst of a dilemma. And there are three simple steps you can follow to do just that:

1. Get clear about the problem.

In order to get the answer you need, you need to understand the problem you're trying to solve. Often, the problem that needs to be addressed in this moment is not about the big picture. It's about a detail you have control over in the big picture. Let's say that fear is overwhelming you because been laid off and need a job, like, yesterday. You may able to snap your fingers and land that new job tomorrow, but you can identify a list of personal contacts to start reaching out to *before* tomorrow with a specific request, such as making an introduction to a decision-maker who can help you reach your bigger goal. Pinpoint the issue. Then address it with very specific, focused action.

2. Ask action questions, probing questions, and expansive questions.

In my book *Listen to Your Life* I identify three types of self-coaching questions. Probing questions help you delve deeper to uncover hidden fears that may be holding you back, such as, "What are you afraid will happen if you move forward?" Expansive questions help you think bigger and start envisioning your dreams: "What would it feel like to double your income in the next 12 months?" Action questions get you moving: "So what's the next step to move you toward that goal, and when will you take it?"

3. Tell the truth.

Lastly, but most importantly, you've got to tell the truth! Coaching is only as effective as you are truthful. Be honest about your fears and your desires, even (especially!) if they scare you. It's the only way to get to the authentic answers that will guide you on the right path—the one that is uniquely meant for you.

My Challenge to You

Start coaching yourself. Ask the right questions and you'll get the right answers.

Coach Yourself

What dilemma are you currently facing? In what situation do you need an answer before you can move forward? What is the most important action question, probing question, and expansive question you need to ask yourself?

_____

_____

_____

_____

_____

_____

_____

_____

_____

_____

_____

_____

What are you putting off?

Even if you're on the right track,
you'll get run over if you just sit there!
Roy Rogers

Point to Ponder:
The instant gratification of conveniences such as e-mail and text
messages stimulate the brain. Break your procrastination-prone
projects into bite-sized goals that allow you to feel you
are making progress.

What have you been putting off? Almost all of us delay necessary actions from time to time. I'm convinced that procrastination is one of the biggest causes of stress in our lives. There is something in your life that you know needs to get done. Often, it's not even something difficult. But you've made it difficult in your mind, and as a result you never get started. Instead, you do everything else you can think of—wash dishes, organize your files, surf the Internet, check e-mail—rather than the thing you actually need to do. Perhaps you're even procrastinating right now. It drains your energy and wastes precious time. "Procrastination is the bad habit of putting off until the day after tomorrow what should have been done the day before yesterday," Napoleon Hill once said.

I challenge you to focus your energy and just do what needs to be done. There are two antidotes to procrastination:

1. **Drop the goal or project, and don't do it.**

2. **Exercise some discipline, and just go ahead and do it.**

Sometimes procrastination is a sign that you don't want or need to do the thing you're dreading, in which case Option 1 is a good choice (this does not apply to filing taxes, paying bills, or picking kids up from school, of course!). At other times, procrastination is a sign of perfectionism, stubbornness, or lack of self-discipline, all of which you have the power to change. If this is the category you relate to, Option 2 is your best choice. Don't make the task or project a big deal. Break it into smaller pieces and just get started.

So what is it that you need to do? Don't wait for inspiration—just start! You don't have to *feel* like doing something to do it. Often, in the process of starting, your mood develops. And even if it doesn't, the feeling of relief after completing a project you've been dreading is well worth it.

My Challenge to You

Stop procrastinating. Get it done!

Coach Yourself

What have you been putting off? How could you break the task into manageable pieces? What step will you take today? By which date will you cross this item off your to-do list?

Instead of being happy *when*, will you be happy *while?*

*I have learned the secret of being content
in any and every situation.*

PHILIPPIANS 4:12

Point to Ponder:

*Research shows that only ten percent of happiness is
determined by your circumstances. Forty percent
is based on what you think and do daily.*

It's an art to remain content with where you are while you're on the way to something better. Do you feel worn out as you race toward the finish line of a goal? We hear the cliché all the time: "It's about the journey, not the destination." But living out the cliché can be a challenge! In a world that values the new and improved it can be tempting to say, "I sure will be happy when I get that new job/my kids graduate/I retire/I win the lottery." But what's even better is being able to say, "I sure will be happy *while* I wait for that new job/my kids are with me/I'm blessed to have a job." Whenever I've noticed a spirit of discontentment rising up to steal my joy, I coach myself with a few questions that help me appreciate the value of here and now.

1. What are you grateful for?

Contentment and gratitude are inextricably connected. Gratitude empowers you to notice the blessings right in front of you. It opens your mind to the little blessings that, if they suddenly disappeared, wouldn't seem so little anymore. Stop talking, thinking, and complaining about what you don't have and start noticing what you do have.

2. What's the most important lesson being offered to you right now?

When you're too focused on the future, you can miss the lesson being offered to you today. Even more important than reaching a goal is who you become in the process of reaching it. What character traits are being developed? What destructive habits are being eliminated? What are you learning that you would not have learned otherwise? Look for the lessons. Appreciate them. Embrace them.

3. When you look back on this time a year from now, what will you wish you had done?

This question is a biggie. When frustration impacts your attitude, you are more likely to make choices you'll later regret. But when you ask yourself this question, you suddenly recognize the magnitude of the opportunity before you. What do you want your legacy to be? Rather than complaining or murmuring about how hard things are, you have an opportunity to face the challenges before you like a champion.

4. In what ways have you already made progress?

Stop taking yourself for granted. Maybe you haven't made perfect progress, but who has? Acknowledge what you have done. Notice your milestones while they are happening. Celebrate them. Treat yourself. Tell the world. Life is happening right now. Rather than waiting to reach the finish line before you mark your progress, do it with every step you take.

My Challenge to You

Choose to be content right now.

Coach Yourself

In what ways do you struggle with a spirit of discontentment? Take some time to consider and respond to the four questions above.

What if it *does* work out?

*Life is a succession of lessons which must
be lived to be understood.*

RALPH WALDO EMERSON

Point to Ponder:

*Trusting God means getting comfortable with
not knowing all the answers.*

Fear. It creeps up on us, often without a sound or a warning. It asks, "What if everything goes wrong?" "What if I fail?" "What if I never get what I want?" And disastrous answers to those questions can send us down a path of negative thinking that spirals out of control. Psychologists call it *catastrophizing*. Next time it happens, stop fear in its path with the opposite question: What if it *does* work out?

What if you succeed? What if you finally get what you want? What if things go right? Asking these questions can give you a sudden burst of energy. That energy is *hope*. It can feel like a small light in a dark place. What if your idea does manifest into all you have hoped? What if that relationship does work out? What if your persistence pays off in spite of your discouragement? What then? Then perhaps it will all have been worth it.

This is not to say you should never have a contingency plan. But you can't live life by simply avoiding your fears. Living and working with passion means giving your all because you believe in the possibility of success. You hold more closely to your dreams and desires than your fears and doubts. So in this moment, I invite you to consider the challenge or possibility that causes you the most doubt or anxiety.

You know the one—that situation that causes the persistent question, "What if it doesn't work out the way I hope?" And then ask the opposite question: "What if it does work out the way I hope?"

Imagine your answer in-depth. Take a moment right now and imagine what it would look like for things to work out. Take a deep breath and close your eyes. What would it feel like? Really imagine yourself there. Imagine the people who are with you. Imagine what you are doing. Imagine how things are different from the way they are in this moment.

Now, move forward focused on the possibilities of your success. Allow your motivation to be a spirit of faith rather than a spirit of fear.

My Challenge to You

Choose optimism. Stop obsessing about what might go wrong and put your energy into what could go right.

Coach Yourself

Consider the thing in your life that you most want but are afraid you will not get. What if it *does* work out? What will that look like? What action can you take that will demonstrate you are operating in faith rather than fear?

Are you in it to win it?

Do you not know that in a race all the runners run,
but only one gets the prize? Run in such a way
as to get the prize.

1 CORINTHIANS 9:24

Point to Ponder:

Having clear, achievable goals is an important
ingredient for a happy life.

I ran across the above Scripture recently. It is one that always inspires me and reminds me of the importance of having a clear goal for my life. It takes discipline, perseverance, and commitment to run the races of life, but the prize at the finish line is so very rewarding. It's not so much about the achievement of your goal as it is about who you become in the process. It can be easy to get stuck in a rut, running your race half-heartedly and with so many distractions that you barely notice there is a higher purpose to what you are doing. I invite you to consider whether you are running your race "in such a way as to get the prize." Whether at work, in your relationships, your finances, your health, or life in general, is it time for you to get motivated again? Consider these four questions to gain the clarity you need.

1. What prize are you aiming for?

Running a race without knowing where the finish line is can be exasperating. Seek clarity about your goal. Aim high. What does winning look like to you? Write it down. A clear, compelling goal is energizing. As the old adage goes, aim for the moon—and if you miss, you'll land among stars.

2. What do you need to do consistently if you are going to win?

Consistency is one of the most important ingredients for success. Perhaps you're aiming for a loving relationship with someone close to you, but you are at odds with the person over petty issues. The relationship seems to be running smoothly for a while, and then an old argument comes up again. Don't give up. Keep practicing love, kindness, patience, and forgiveness. Don't keep a record of wrongs. Over time, the consistency of your love will pay off. Whether building a relationship or losing weight, consistent action toward your goal will eventually yield results.

3. Why is it important to you?

Discipline without purpose is self-punishment. Indeed, self-control is one of the fruits the Holy Spirit helps us to produce in our lives (Galatians 5:23) for the purpose of becoming all that we were meant to be. But denying yourself constantly without the reward of moving toward a larger objective is frustrating. Know the core purpose behind the race you are running. If you are seeking better health by eating well and exercising, the purpose may simply be to live long and feel your best. If you are seeking financial independence, the purpose may be to have the freedom to spend less time working and more time enjoying people and exploring life.

4. Why is it important to God?

Ultimately, the prize you are aiming for is becoming all that God called you to be and fulfilling the purpose for which you were created. In every race, seek to grow spiritually, express love, and embrace the lessons that are being offered to you. If you do these three things, the matchless prize you'll earn are the words "Well done, good and faithful servant!" (Matthew 25:21).

My Challenge to You

Make a decision that you will run your race with a goal of winning it. If there are any "races" you are running aimlessly, either get out of that race altogether or get clear about the prize you are seeking.

Coach Yourself

What is the prize you most want to attain at this point in your life? (Consider your health, relationships, finances, work, and spiritual life.) What do you need to do differently in order to win it? Why is it important to you? Why is it important to God?

_____

_____

_____

_____

_____

_____

_____

_____

In what way is it time to stretch yourself?

When you stretch outside your comfort zone,
don't be surprised when you feel uncomfortable.
The longer you stay in that new zone, the
more comfortable you will become.

Valorie Burton

Point to Ponder:

Studies show we fear an unknown outcome more than we
fear a known bad outcome. But in order to try something
new, we must overcome our fear of the unknown.

As you begin to make changes in your life, don't burden yourself with a long list of goals. Instead, get inspired. Set a goal that stretches you and, as a result, excites you enough that you are spurred to action. A "stretch goal" develops your character by tapping into and cultivating your strengths.

It starts with asking yourself the right questions. Here are a few questions to help you find your own stretch goal. Answer them to find the inspiration to forge ahead and stick to that goal:

1. What vision feels just beyond your reach?

It might be something you see for other people, but for whatever reason you don't see it for yourself—even though you want it. Maybe it's an income double or triple what you make now. Perhaps it's exploring your romantic streak or your fun side. It may even be your dream of being disciplined enough to eat healthy and exercise. The goal here is not to choose something that's realistic, necessarily, but to choose something that feels beyond your reach—as though it's not really possible for you. *But it is possible.* Do you have the faith to believe it? A stretch goal is one that forces you to reach higher than you think you can. If you don't have to stretch for it, it's not big enough for this exercise.

2. What specific, measurable, and time-sensitive goal would bring you closer to that vision?

Now for the fun part. Get specific about the goal. Make it vivid. Describe it in a way that allows you to measure your progress and know when you have reached the finish line. And most importantly, give yourself a deadline. You know what happens when there's no deadline, right? It's always something you'll start tomorrow. Before you know it, a year has passed and you set the same goal again! "I'm going to have more fun and truly enjoy my life rather than treating every activity like a burden" is a great vision. You could break that down by saying, "I am going to travel for pleasure more. Once every three months I am going to take a fun trip, even if it's just a weekend road trip somewhere adventurous. And my first trip will be four weeks from now."

3. Whom will you tell?

Don't keep your vision and goal to yourself. Tell somebody. In fact, tell multiple people—supportive people. Negative people tend to throw water on your passion and excitement: "Are you sure?" "That sounds hard." "You've never done that before!" You don't need those comments. Find someone encouraging—someone who may even want to do this exercise with you. Don't keep it to yourself so you can quietly drop the goal if you don't achieve it. Commit to it. Declare it out loud. Sharing your plans with others makes it far more likely that you'll actually carry them out.

My Challenge to You

Stop playing it safe. Stretch!

Coach Yourself

What vision feels just beyond your reach? What specific, measurable, and time-sensitive goal would bring you closer to that vision? Whom will you tell?

_____

_____

_____

_____

_____

_____

_____

_____

_____

_____

_____

_____

What is your procrastination telling you?

For a dream comes through much activity,
and a fool's voice is known by his many words.
ECCLESIASTES 5:3 NKJV

Point to Ponder:

The recurring themes in your life reveal the truth about what
issues you most need to address. Listen for the lesson.

In my struggles as a recovering procrastinator, I have learned a simple lesson: You can look extremely productive while producing not much of anything. In the name of planning, we procrastinate. We analyze, plan, research, mull over, and consider. Then we analyze some more, plan some more, and research some more. It is as if we expect things to magically come together if we just think about them hard enough. Maybe you've been there—or perhaps you're there right now.

The truth is, you don't reach your dreams by overthinking. You reach your dreams by *doing*. Stop planning and start doing. Don't worry about doing it perfectly, or having it all figured out. That's never going to happen anyway. Give yourself permission to be imperfect. Trust that if you make a mistake you can learn from it, make adjustments, and keep moving forward.

When you find yourself procrastinating, dig deep to see what's really going on. Often procrastination isn't about simply putting off a difficult task. It is about the counterproductive thoughts that can sabotage your success. Some of these thoughts are ones you are not consciously aware of. But if you become more aware of these thoughts—and intentionally change them to something more productive—you can get unstuck and become unstoppable.

Are you holding back? Are you stuck in neutral, not moving forward on plans you say you want to see come to pass? If so, you have to wonder what's really keeping you stuck. It's probably not just that you have too much on your to-do list today or the distraction of text messages or e-mail or social media. Truth be told, when you really want something, you take action. You don't let anything get in the way.

As you look at the five revealing subconscious thoughts many procrastinators have, be honest with yourself. Do any of these thoughts resonate?

1. **"Truth is, I like things just the way they are."**

   Sometimes you think you should do something, but you really don't want to do it. You like things the way they are. Maybe you need to give yourself permission to stay where you are— or maybe it's time to muster the courage to shake things up a bit. The choice is yours. Just don't stay in that inauthentic place of insisting you want something you are never actually going to pursue.

2. **"Tackling the project at hand is too complicated."**

   Many procrastinators tell themselves that the task at hand is complicated. Because it's complicated, they feel overwhelmed or paralyzed. They can't even get started. Do you do that? Break the task down into specific action steps—one at a time. What is the next step you could take right now? Do that.

3. **"I don't really think I deserve to have what I want."**

   This statement is one that gets to the heart of your self-esteem. Whether you feel guilty about something you did in the past or you don't feel worthy for some reason, you won't move forward if you don't believe you should have the thing you want. Subconsciously, you can sabotage your success by procrastinating. Do you really believe you deserve to have the goal you say you're aiming for?

4. "I don't really think it can happen."

One of the most basic and necessary elements of goal setting is self-efficacy—your belief that you can accomplish the goal. Without that belief, what's the point of putting forth effort? A lack of confidence can be masked as procrastination. Be honest. Do you need to strengthen your belief that it is possible to fulfill your dream?

5. "I'm afraid of what others will think, say, or do."

Fear is at the root of most self-sabotaging behaviors. Are you willing to allow what others think (or what you're afraid they might think) to control you? Make an intentional decision.

My Challenge to You

Peel back the layers and uncover the real culprit of your procrastination.

Coach Yourself

After considering the root of your procrastination, take a look at the five self-sabotaging thoughts above and ask yourself, "Which of these are true for me?" Is the thought helping you or hurting you? Are you willing to change it? If so, what new thought do you want to embrace that will empower you to finally move forward?

Who are you *really*?

Be yourself. Everyone else is taken.

Oscar Wilde

Point to Ponder:

Authenticity is a hallmark of resilience.

In recent conversations, the theme "be yourself" has come up several times. And when themes emerge, I always like to seek the lesson for myself and eventually share it. If you feel like sometimes you struggle with saying what you mean, doing what you love, or relaxing around certain people, then this message is especially for you. Yet even if you are confident and sure that you are comfortable being yourself, there is often room to go a little deeper—an opportunity to uncover another layer of authenticity and free yourself to be unapologetically you.

Not being at ease with yourself just as you are is exhausting. You might not even realize the amount of energy that is being drained by keeping up appearances, attempting to be perfect, pleasing other people, and trying to make yourself fit into situations that are simply not you. The notion of "being yourself" can feel a little vague, so consider these five practical strategies that will help you maximize your best you:

1. Say what you need to say.

Are you beating around the bush? Too afraid to speak up? Have you found yourself telling a little lie to avoid the embarrassment of telling the truth? That's a clear sign you are not being true to yourself. Identify at least one situation in which you have not said what you need to say. When you finish reading this, go to the person who needs to hear it and just say it. If you can't say it now, then mark your calendar for the date and time when you will. Authenticity means being forthright. Don't waste precious energy pretending all is well when it isn't.

2. Wear what makes you feel your best.

It may seem superficial, but it's not. Clothing is a language all its own. What does yours say about you? And is that message consistent with who you truly are? When I transitioned from running a public relations firm that focused on corporate clients to my current work in personal and spiritual growth, I changed my daily wardrobe. Out with the suits (which I thought made me look more mature and credible since I was in my twenties then) and in with a more relaxed, fun look. But truth be told, even at the beginning of my career I could have cultivated a wardrobe that was relaxed and fun while still being professional. It takes some creativity, but you can dress in a way that makes you feel good even when your clothing choices are restricted for professional reasons.

3. Do what you know is right.

There is nothing more authentic than living your values. When your actions don't line up with your beliefs, inner turmoil is sure to follow. Do what's right and you'll have a sense of peace about your decisions and actions.

4. Give yourself permission to be imperfect.

When we are uncomfortable in our own skin, most of the time it is because we haven't given ourselves permission to be human. In other words, we haven't given ourselves permission to be imperfect. When you relax, you enjoy yourself more. When you value the journey as much as, if not more than, the destination, you embrace the fact that there will be bumps along the road—but they don't have to keep you from reaching your purpose.

5. Breathe.

Whenever you feel yourself getting anxious, take a deep breath. Let the air in and out slowly. Breathe and get centered again. It's such a simple concept that can make an immense improvement in your life and daily well-being—just like being yourself.

My Challenge to You

Be yourself!

Coach Yourself

In what situations (work, home, with friends, at church, etc.) are you most likely not to be yourself? What are you afraid will happen if you show people the real you? What specifically do you do or say that does not represent who you really are? When will you stop doing that? Will you try today?

_____

_____

_____

_____

_____

_____

_____

What lesson is life offering you right now?

In the book of life, the answers aren't in the back.
CHARLIE BROWN

Point to Ponder:
*Regularly writing down your thoughts, ideas, and lessons
learned can boost your feelings of contentment.*

I challenge you to consider the lessons your life is offering you right now. I say *offering* because God offers lessons, but it is up to us to learn from them. If we don't learn, the same lessons will be offered again and again. Through both frustrations and exciting times, there is something for you to learn that will prepare you for greater opportunities on your horizon. Today, I want you to be intentional about looking for those lessons and finding ways to apply them to the daily challenges you face.

Here are five of the greatest lessons I have learned on my journey thus far. Perhaps you've learned or encountered these along your journey as well. If so, consider these a reminder today:

1. Nothing is permanent.

I first learned this lesson at the age of six, which was the first time my family moved. We left my birthplace of Florida and moved to Germany. I moved eight more times by the time I turned twenty-one—to cities in Colorado, South Carolina, California, back to Florida, and Texas. Growing up in an Air Force family, I quickly learned to adapt to new circumstances, new people, and sometimes even a new country. Nothing in life is permanent—a fact that should encourage you to revel in the joy your life is bringing *right now* and minimize your frustration when you encounter circumstances you don't like. There is something in your life right now that is not permanent. If it is something you love, in what ways could you embrace and enjoy it more? If it is something you don't think you can handle, just hold on a little longer. This too shall pass.

2. You are either living on purpose or living by accident.

Too many people wander through life haphazardly—latching onto acquaintances, jobs, and life situations just because they crossed their path. Those people are bound to wake up one day wondering, "How on earth did I get here?" I call this *living by accident*. In order to create a fulfilling life, you have to be purposeful in your decisions. Don't make a decision without reflecting on what long-term impact it will have on you and the people you love. Pursue the things that empower you to express your values and talents. Choose to be around people you feel good being around—inspiring, supportive people who are moving in the same direction you are. Know your purpose and live in it every day in your work, relationships, health, finances, and spiritual life. Strive not to end up anywhere by accident—just because it was convenient.

3. Fear does not necessarily mean *stop.*

Fear is as powerful as you allow it to be. Most of us feel fear and interpret that feeling as a warning to stop moving forward. In truth, we should interpret most fear as a natural emotion that pops up every time we venture to do something outside of our comfort zone. When you feel fear, keep moving. It'll stretch you beyond your comfort zone and get you closer to your goals. What are you afraid of right now that is keeping you from living your best life? Will you make a decision to move forward despite your fear?

4. Less is more.

More than ever, our culture is fixated on proving your worth through your money and material possessions. Whole television shows are dedicated to showing you all the "stuff" other people have. After a while it can be pretty challenging not to compare your stuff to everyone else's! But true self-empowerment comes from knowing that nothing material will ever prove your worth. Your worth comes from your identity as a child of God and the impact you make in the lives of others. Don't worry about impressing everyone else. Instead, focus on impressing God by living the purpose for which He created you—serving and blessing others in the way that only you can.

5. The power to change your life is in the choices you make.

This is perhaps the most powerful of lessons. Better choices create better circumstances. It's not what happens to you that most impacts your life. It is how you respond. Your choices create your future. What kind of future are you creating with the choices you are making today? You can choose to enjoy your life or to be miserable. You can choose to be flexible or keep hitting a brick wall at work or in a relationship. You can choose to pursue your dreams or keep making excuses for why you can't achieve them. The choice is yours.

My Challenge to You

From the list of five lessons above, choose the one that you most need to apply to your life right now. Make a decision to take an action in the next 48 hours that will enrich your life in a positive, meaningful way.

Coach Yourself

What is the most important lesson *your* life is offering you right now? How will you apply this lesson in your future?

Is it time to stop trying to figure it out?

If any of you lacks wisdom, you should ask God,
who gives generously to all without finding fault,
and it will be given to you.

JAMES 1:5

Point to Ponder:

Being okay with the fact that sometimes there is
no solution—at least not right now—can be
a key to contentment.

My mother loves to tell the story that when I was two years old, I taught myself how to tie my shoes. I'd asked her several times to teach me. Although she said she'd teach me when I got bigger, I insisted that she show me how to do it. So she did. One afternoon she spent 45 minutes patiently demonstrating shoe-tying step by step as I diligently attempted to follow her instructions. But I couldn't get it, and I became very frustrated. "Baby, you're too young," she said in a comforting, motherly tone. "We'll try again when you get a little older," she promised, leaving me in my bedroom to play while she went to cook dinner. Apparently I didn't do much playing, she recalls. To her utter astonishment, I emerged from my room an hour later—shoes perfectly tied. When she asked how I did it, I replied in my then-Southern drawl, "I jes figgiditout!" (Translation: "I just figured it out!")

Throughout my childhood, it became a phrase I'd use whenever I figured something out on my own. But as I entered adulthood and began to grow spiritually, I noticed that figuring things out isn't always as easy as just deciding to do so. Not everything in life is as simple as "just figuring it out." Of course, there are definitely times in life when your determination to understand something is essential. Perseverance is the key to your success when you set out to live a purposeful life. However, there are some things in life that we can waste our energy trying to figure out. It is in those situations that we must be willing to let go, pray for wisdom, and trust God.

Identify the things in your life that you have been fruitlessly trying to figure out. Here are a few of the most common:

- **When "the one" will come into your life so you can get married.**
- **Why something happened that you wish had not occurred.**
- **Why you are trying to figure out and fix someone else's problem.**
- **When a long-awaited door will open in your life.**
- **Why some people are blessed in certain ways that others are not.**
- **Why it's taking longer than you anticipated to see your dream come true.**

In what area of your life do you find yourself frustrated and trying to figure out something that perhaps is not meant to be figured out? Doing so consistently can lead you to be stuck, angry, or aggravated with God. "Trust in the LORD with all your heart and lean not on your own understanding," Proverbs 3:5 reminds us. Sometimes our knowledge is too limited to figure out why things happen (or don't happen) the way they do. God sees the big picture. Our job is to trust completely. You can learn to accept a difficult situation while continually learning and growing spiritually.

When you don't know what to do or how to deal with certain situations, ask for wisdom. Stop trying to figure it out. Let go of the need to control when and how a situation will resolve itself. Take a deep breath. Pray for wisdom. Then slow down and get quiet enough to hear that still, small voice whisper words of comfort, peace, and wisdom into your spirit.

My Challenge to You

Identify what you need to stop trying to figure out. Let it go. Pray and listen for wisdom about how to proceed from here.

Coach Yourself

In what current life situations do you need to let go of control and trust God more? When and how will you begin to do that?

_____

_____

_____

_____

_____

_____

_____

_____

_____

_____

Will you give yourself permission to make a change?

Nobody can go back and start a new beginning, but anyone can start today and make a new ending.

Maria Robinson

Point to Ponder:

Engaging in work and activities that are meaningful for you is a key to greater personal fulfillment.

During a radio interview, a caller in her forties asked me if it was too late to change careers and pursue something she was more passionate about. "It's never too late," I told her. "If you feel led in a new direction, make a plan to transition and go for it!"

Her call came as no surprise. Many people I've encountered over the years—some in their twenties, others in their sixties—have sent me letters and e-mails wondering if it's too late to make a change. Is it too late to change jobs? Is it too late to save a relationship? Is it too late to start planning for retirement?

I challenge you to let go of the idea that it's too late to change the course of your life. In a world that pressures us to believe everything must happen in a compressed time frame, it can feel as though it is "against the rules" to follow a path that is outside the norm. It can especially feel like it is unacceptable to change your mind about what you want in life. But God will often lead you in a new direction once you've learned all that you were supposed to learn at a particular stage in your life.

Your experiences have developed you into a unique person whose path does not look like anyone else's—nor should it. Even when you've made mistakes, it is not too late to learn from them and make a change for the better.

What have you previously decided it was too late for you to do? Is it time to reconsider? Let this message rekindle your desire for change. Give yourself permission to dream a bigger dream and walk a divinely inspired path that is uniquely your own. Remember, it's *not* too late to try something new. In fact, life becomes stagnant when you get stuck in a rut. It's tempting to give up on the idea that you could have what you really want in your life, but you don't have to give in to that temptation. Your journey becomes richer and more joyful when you remain open to your possibilities.

Here are a few things it's not too late for you to do. Add a few items of your own if you wish.

- **Change careers**

- **Go back to school**

- **Fall in love**

- **Apologize to someone you hurt**

- **Forgive someone who hurt you**

- **Plan a trip to your dream destination**

- **Have children (even if it's biologically impossible, the child you were meant to have may be waiting to be adopted by you)**

- **Start saving for retirement**

- **Get fit**

- **Start taking better care of yourself**

- **Turn your finances around**

- **Deepen your relationship with God**

- **Change your attitude or your perspective on life**

- _____

- _____

- _____

My Challenge to You

Make a decision to open your mind to new possibilities. Take a step in the direction of your potential.

Coach Yourself

What have you decided it's too late to do? How would it feel for you to experience that opportunity after all? What will you do to move toward it?

_____

_____

_____

_____

_____

Is God trying to tell you something?

Every once in a while you need to be quiet and listen for the guidance of that still, small voice.

Valorie Burton

Point to Ponder:

Research shows that religious people—those who believe in God—are happier and more skilled at bouncing back from major setbacks.

Every once in a while, when a similar message keeps crossing my path or a door refuses to open no matter how hard I pry, the song "God Is Trying to Tell You Something" will bubble up in my spirit. It happened to me this week as I noticed that I was humming the tune under my breath. I couldn't help but log in to YouTube to watch the famous scene from my favorite movie, *The Color Purple*, in which the song marks a pivotal point in the story line.

Perhaps today, you're reading this page because there is a message God is trying to send to you too. Is there a problem that keeps recurring, a theme that keeps showing up in your work or life, or a message that has been communicated through multiple people that it's time for you to acknowledge? It can be tempting to ignore messages we don't want to hear, or to take for granted the positive messages that come through other people. But it's important to be open to life's messages in their various forms. Sometimes the message is a warning— "Stop that." Sometimes it's a nudge—"Get ready." At other times, it's an encouragement—"You're on the right path." Whatever the message, your job is to listen.

In order to listen, we need to be open and sensitive to messages. Often, events in our lives are not simply coincidences. Here are a few ways God might be trying to tell you something:

- **The same issue keeps showing up again and again—maybe it's time to address it.**

- **You don't feel at peace about a situation in your life. There may be a message in the turmoil.**

- **You do feel at peace. There is a message in that too.**

- **A similar idea or theme keeps showing up—perhaps there is something to learn.**

- **You're having trouble taking constructive criticism, instead making excuses for areas of your life where there is room for improvement.**

- **A door has closed in some area of your life. Perhaps there is something better or different on the horizon.**

My Challenge to You

Pay attention to the messages that show up repeatedly in your life.

Coach Yourself

What has God been trying to tell you lately? What do you need to do as a result of that message?

What's your mission?

Here is the test to find whether your mission on Earth is finished. If you're alive, it isn't.

RICHARD BACH

Point to Ponder:

Finding meaning and purpose in your life is essential for experiencing true fulfillment and happiness.

I was speaking in Saskatoon, a city I'd never heard of until the conference organizers called. It sounded like the name of Bugs Bunny's hometown, but I discovered it was a real city in Saskatchewan, Canada. It was a cold November day, but the smiling and nodding from a woman in the audience sitting about ten rows back toward the right side of the stage warmed my heart. I'll never forget her. She nodded, laughed, and even nudged her girlfriend next to her every time I made a great point. I spoke three times that day to a conference of 1,200 women and she shone like a bright light, giving me a boost of energy and confidence every time I looked her way. During my book signing at the end of the day, she came through the line.

"I remember you!" I said, happy to have a chance to meet and thank her. "You were sitting in about the tenth row, a little to my right."

Shocked that I had noticed her in the audience and actually remembered where she was sitting, she said, "Do you remember where everyone in the audience sat?"

"No, I sure don't. But I remember you. Every time I looked your way you were smiling and energetic. Let me ask you something. Is it your mission to bring joy to people?" I said.

She looked both perplexed and elated. "Can my mission really be that simple?" she asked. "People at work tell me I bring them joy all the time! I've been trying to figure out what my mission is. I didn't know it could be that simple!"

Your mission is not complicated. It is a simple, one-sentence description. And if you have not yet articulated it, know this: Your mission is to love and serve others using your gifts, strengths, and resources. So until you get clear about the specifics, embrace that as your mission and I guarantee you'll be on the right track.

My Challenge to You

Get clear about your personal mission or purpose. Then be intentional about living it.

Coach Yourself

What's your purpose or personal mission? If you could sum it up in one sentence, how would you articulate it? It answers this simple question: How is someone's life better because they cross your path?

What was the best thing that happened to you today?

Be thankful for what you have; you'll end up having more. If you concentrate on what you don't have, you will never, ever have enough.

OPRAH WINFREY

Point to Ponder:

The positive emotion generated by your expressions of gratitude can boost your immune system and make you physically healthier.

This is one of my favorite questions to ask people in lieu of the overused and often insincere, "How are you?" It's a simple but thought-provoking question. Ask it of others—and once a day, ask it of yourself. In my seminars and workshops, I often have participants ask each other, "What's the best thing that's happened to you today (or this week or this month)?" Most people have to think for a moment, but the response is always one that lifts the spirits and puts life in a whole new perspective.

It can be easy to get so busy that you forget to notice the good things going on in your life. Sure, maybe your job or your finances aren't where you want them to be, but something great is happening with your family or friends. Celebrate it! Acknowledge it! Gratitude is the first step toward ensuring that joy permeates your life on a daily basis.

Over the coming week or month, I challenge you to celebrate your life by noticing the milestones, wins, and good things that are happening in your life. At the end of each day, ask yourself, "What was the best thing that happened to me today?" Jot down your responses. Then, at the end of the week, choose the best thing that's happened all week and come up with a fun way to celebrate it.

So often in life we move too quickly to truly enjoy the good things that come our way. But why not make celebrating your life, especially the good things in your life, a regular habit? If you finally got started on the exercise plan you've been talking about for months, do something fun for yourself to celebrate taking a step toward a healthier lifestyle. If someone else blessed you in some way and that was the best thing that's happened all week, celebrate by finding a creative way to be a blessing to them. If you finally got around to clearing your clutter, celebrate your newfound space! Find ways to celebrate your progress and life will become something to smile about—every single day.

My Challenge to You

Notice the good things in life and celebrate them! Choose at least one good thing to celebrate over the next week.

Coach Yourself

Look back over the last year. What are the best things that have happened to you? What makes you feel grateful and excited about life? Noticing the things that are good about your life often gives you the fuel to keep pushing forward, even on the days when things don't quite go your way.

Is it time for a fresh start?

You wouldn't wear a wool coat in July or flip-flops in a blizzard. When a new season arrives, walk into it dressed and ready for what's coming.
VALORIE BURTON

Point to Ponder:
People who try new things are happier than people who always hold on to what's familiar.

Every year I get giddy when the first signs of spring whisper promises of winter's demise. Sure, it might get cold again. It could even snow. But it won't last! If I can just hang on a little while longer, spring is certain to arrive.

Our lives have seasons too. If you're not careful, you can stay stuck in an old season when a new one arrives. When your life is cluttered with unnecessary distractions, tolerations, or just plain junk, it can feel impossible to find your way forward. But you must make room for what you want.

Do you need to clear out the clutter today? Use these five coaching questions to make room for a new season:

1. **What project/issue/to-do list item keeps getting rolled over to the next season?**
   You know what I'm talking about. It's the thing you keep saying you're going to do, but don't. You procrastinate. Declare

you will get started, then forget. Or maybe you hope it will just go away. Whatever the case, make a decision to either do it or drop it. Which will it be?

2. What could you de-clutter in the next 15 minutes?

When it comes to clearing clutter and making space for something new in your life, it can be tempting to make it too big a deal in your head, which means you'll keep putting it off for later. Instead, get the energy moving by getting rid of some of the clutter in your environment. Transforming your physical space is often a catalyst for transforming your inner space. Set a timer for 15 minutes and pick up everything you can before the alarm goes off. Put away the books and magazines you left out and file that pile of mail you've been avoiding! You'll be amazed at how much you can accomplish.

3. What ties need to be cut?

Is there a relationship, whether with a person or organization, that it is time to end? Making room in your life often means letting go of stale or inauthentic connections.

4. What apology is overdue?

Don't go into a new season with old baggage. If you are holding on to something—a grudge, bitterness, anger—choose today to let it go. It is a heavy burden to carry, and even if you think the other person is responsible, in truth, you bear the burden alone. Depending on the situation, either forgive or ask for forgiveness.

5. How do I want to use this season to prepare for the next?

Wise people think about the upcoming season while still in the present one. This enables them to lay the groundwork for a smooth transition. The next season of your life is already on its way. Is there anything you need to do now to prepare?

My Challenge to You

Change is coming! Clear some space for what you want to see show up in the next season of your life.

Coach Yourself

Take some time to consider and respond to the five questions above.

_____

_____

_____

_____

_____

_____

_____

_____

_____

_____

_____

Is it time for a break?

It is our best work that God wants, not the dregs of our exhaustion. I think he must prefer quality to quantity.
George MacDonald

Point to Ponder:
Taking breaks makes you more productive. So stop working through lunch. Give your mind a break. You'll be better for it.

Do you need a break? Many of us do, but the real question is whether or not you'll take time for one. Those of us alive today are living at a faster pace than any human beings who've ever walked the planet. Advertisers tell us our tech gadgets will save us time, but as quickly as we save it, we raise our expectations about how much we can accomplish with the time we have left. It's like being on a treadmill and slowly but consistently increasing the speed. Sure, you're running faster. You're getting it done. But at some point, you just want to get off the treadmill! Here are a few signs it's time to take a break.

1. **You are busy but not productive.**

   You know what I'm talking about. You're doing stuff, just not the most important stuff. You're moving, but not progressing. If that's you, take a break. Refocus. Restart.

2. **You are irritable, even when nothing particularly stressful is happening.**

   If your attitude at work is always sour no matter what, there's something simmering beneath the surface. Anger—including the quiet, passive-aggressive type—is usually a sign that a boundary has been crossed. Resentment emerges when we don't speak up, ask for help, or make a necessary change.

3. You just accomplished a big goal.

Research shows that our energy is depleted after the accomplishment of a big goal. We are more effective at meeting future goals when we give our minds and bodies a chance to recover so that our energy will be replenished for the next big task at hand. Just finished a major project? Celebrate. Relax. Rejuvenate. Then move on to the next big thing.

4. Your body hurts.

Your body will give you warning signs. Don't ignore them. Chronic back or neck pain, headaches, and fatigue are just a few of the ways your body is trying to talk to you. Listen. If you don't, there could be long-term consequences ahead.

5. You're dreaming about work.

If you are dreaming about projects, deadlines, and that pesky coworker, it's a definite sign that some downtime is overdue.

6. You haven't had a break in a while.

Even if none of the other five signs are relevant to you right now, you still need regular breaks. If you haven't taken one recently, get going! Ten minutes every couple of hours, a day of downtime every week, and a vacation or personal days for fun time every few months will make you far more productive—and far happier—than working nonstop.

My Challenge to You

Give yourself a break!

Coach Yourself

What are some signs you have begun to exhibit that indicate you need a break? What do you need a break from? When will you take that break?

_____

_____

_____

_____

_____

_____

_____

_____

_____

_____

_____

_____

_____

_____

Is impatience sabotaging your potential?

He who knows patience knows peace.
CHINESE PROVERB

Point to Ponder:
Patience can be developed with practice.

What goal or desire are you rushing toward? What is it that you just can't wait to see unfold in your life? It often seems the thing we want most can take the longest to manifest. And while we're waiting, it can be tempting to try making something happen—find a solution to your problem or desire that almost fits, but not quite. It may be time to practice patience as the next step to moving forward in your life.

A lack of patience is often a sign of fear, and fear of waiting can sabotage your biggest goals. We want what we want *now*, so we get anxious and worried and start pushing for things to happen before their time. Slow down. Trust. Breathe. Patience is an act of faith, even when you don't know when or how things will work out. Consider the key areas of your life. In what ways do you need to practice more patience?

Relationships

Are you short-tempered with people? Irritated when you have to wait in line at the store? Impatient with someone who is trying, but just doesn't live up to your expectations? Or scared the relationship of your dreams will never be a reality? If you are single and want to be married, one of the biggest mistakes you can ever make is to turn a relationship into more than it was meant to be. Out of fear that another will not come along, that you're getting too old to be married, or that your options are limited, you might be tempted to marry the wrong person. Don't do it. Be patient. Trust. Often, just when you relax about it, the door to love will open.

Work

At work, a lack of patience can sabotage your relationships with coworkers or customers and even keep you from putting your skills to use. You've got to put in the time before you can advance. As a result, you may be tempted to hop from job to job without establishing momentum in your career.

Finances

I am convinced that the leading cause of consumer debt is a lack of patience. I know this was the case in my twenties when I racked up credit card debt instead of saving for the things I really wanted. A sense of entitlement can cause us to buy things on credit because we think we deserve them—even if we can't afford them. A little patience in fulfilling your material desires might help you rein in that spending.

Health

If there is one thing that takes patience and perseverance, it's eating healthy and exercising. The results come slowly and take time before they're noticeable—which is why diet pills and fad diets are a multi-billion-dollar industry! Are you looking for shortcuts to good health? There aren't any. Make a commitment to start making changes one at a time and you'll build up good habits that lead to good health and better looks.

My Challenge to You

Practice patience. Good things do come to those who wait.

Coach Yourself

In what ways do you need to be more patient this week? What

are you afraid will happen if you have to wait longer than you want to? What will it take for you to let go of that fear?

Are you overwhelmed with too many goals?

There are many good opportunities you could take advantage of. But then you have little time for the one great opportunity before you.

VALORIE BURTON

Point to Ponder:

Research shows we can suffer from "decision fatigue." It takes energy to pursue goals and make decisions to achieve them. Overcome goal fatigue by taking a moment to celebrate your wins and replenish your energy for the next goal.

Maybe you're motivated to make some changes in your life, and you've set yourself a long list of goals. But that list of things you're trying to change can feel overwhelming! We become depleted after exerting the self-regulation it takes to make a change. This is called "goal fatigue." Perhaps you can relate. No sooner than you reach one milestone, you get focused on the next. No time to celebrate. No time to get reenergized. Attempting to change everything in your life at once can be overwhelming. It's not that you shouldn't have a vision for transformation. Just be sensitive to the overload and discouragement that can creep in when you expect yourself to run at full speed in every area of your life. You can have multiple goals, but be strategic about how much energy you allocate to each at any given time. Here's how.

1. Identify a handful of key goals for the next 12 months.

In your case, you might choose to position yourself for a new career by pursuing new assignments at work that will expand your skills. Maybe you'll create a goal of arriving at a healthy weight (as determined by your doctor) by the summer, or to increase your income by a specific amount by this time next year.

2. Ask yourself, "What is the most important habit I need to develop (or eliminate) in order to reach my goal?"

When it comes to actually bringing your goal to fruition, it's about what you do every day. Rather than focusing on the goal, identify the most important habit that would lead to the fulfillment of the goal. As Aristotle once said, "We are what we repeatedly do." If you want to lose 30 pounds but you eat greasy takeout most nights at 9:30 p.m., it's going to be hard. So create a new habit: Eat a light, healthy dinner at 6:30 p.m. every night. Focus on that as your one goal for the next month. Likewise, if you own a part-time business and want to increase your revenue, create a sales habit—like daily outreach to at least three customers.

3. As you conquer each habit, add a new one.

Once your new habit becomes an old one, focus on the next habit you want to develop in order to reach one of your goals. Continue this throughout the year.

4. Make yourself accountable.

Mark your habit-forming plans on your calendar throughout the year. Decide now which habit you'll be working on several months from now, and have a system to remind yourself. And tell others about your plans! You are far more likely to accomplish something when you don't keep it to yourself. Otherwise, without any family, friends, or coworkers available to keep you accountable, you'll be more likely to drop the goal when the going gets tough. Put yourself out there. Declare your goals! Tell the world. Then you'll have some positive pressure to live up to them.

My Challenge to You

Avoid goal fatigue.

Coach Yourself

In what ways are you overwhelmed and experiencing goal fatigue? What would feel like a more workable plan?

Do you know the five keys to negotiation?

Let us never negotiate out of fear.
But let us never fear to negotiate.
JOHN F. KENNEDY

Point to Ponder:
*Doing your homework and using facts or statistics to back up
your requests will give you an advantage.*

Does the idea of asking for a raise make you squeamish? Does the idea of negotiating for a better price make you want to run in the other direction? Are you charging the same for your services that you charged ten years ago, afraid to tell your clients you're raising your rates? Whether you finally got the job offer you were looking for, have the opportunity for a promotion at work, or are angling for some flex time, knowing how to negotiate will help you get more of what you want. The most important question you can ask is, "How could I make this a better deal for me and the other side?" Use these five strategies to help you negotiate like a pro:

1. Speak last.

In a negotiation, do your best to get the other side to make the first offer. Why? First, they may offer more than you were anticipating and you'll shoot yourself in the foot if you speak first and ask for less. Better to allow the other side to speak first.

2. Don't be afraid to ask.

Most people never negotiate because they're too scared to ask.

Get over it—and this is especially important for women, who disproportionately accept the initial offer. You'll be surprised what you can negotiate simply by asking.

3. Know the range of what you're looking for.

The key to a good negotiation is to have some degree of flexibility. So have a range and know the number you are not willing to fall beneath. You need to know your bottom line before going into a negotiation. At what point are you willing to walk away?

4. Do your homework.

If you're negotiating your salary, know what the job is worth. Understand your value and communicate it specifically and clearly. If you have examples of situations in which what you are proposing worked, use those examples to make your point.

5. Make a goodwill gesture.

How you negotiate says a lot about you. A good negotiation, especially with an employer or client, is one in which both parties can leave feeling they got something good for their side. "Winner takes all" is a losing strategy for your career. Leave something on the table. What are you willing to give as a goodwill gesture? If you're negotiating for flex time, are you willing to be on call? If you are negotiating a salary, are you willing to budge at all?

My Challenge to You

Be bold. Get over your fear of negotiating!

Coach Yourself

Where are you possibly selling yourself short? In what way do you want better terms and what step will you take in that direction?

What would help you push through to your breakthrough?

In the confrontation between the stream and the rock, the stream always wins—not through strength but by perseverance.

H. Jackson Brown

Point to Ponder:

Resilience is a skill that can be learned. It begins with your ability to become more aware and intentional about what you say to yourself when faced with adversity.

Whether your career feels stagnant or a relationship is in a rut, we all get stuck from time to time. One of the differences between those who are truly fulfilled in life and those who aren't is the ability to push through tough times to get to the other side. I've been there and done that—and helped many of my clients do it too. Being stuck doesn't have to mean staying stuck. Here are three ways you can get out of that rut and start to move on with your life.

1. Be at peace with frustration.

Life doesn't always feel good—and that's not necessarily a bad thing. Sometimes there is simply no getting around feeling sad, frustrated, or even angry. Give your negative emotions permission to exist so they can run their course. This doesn't mean you have to *act* on those emotions. It simply means you don't ignore and suppress them to your own detriment. Your emotions are like a clogged drain. The only way to get unclogged is to let the gunk wash through. Eventually, the drain will clear and the water will flow free.

2. Take a step forward.

The key to getting unstuck is to build momentum. Once you get moving it's easier to *keep* moving. But don't overwhelm yourself with a myriad of action steps. Instead, choose one doable step in the right direction. What could you do today to get you unstuck? For example, if you've fallen off your diet, give away that bag of cookies you just bought at the vending machine. Then stop by the grocery store tonight to pick up a few healthy snacks to put in your desk. Those will help you fight that four o'clock candy bar temptation tomorrow. If you've nearly given up on that job search, make a phone call to that person who said they might be able to help. Reaching out to others is a powerful step forward—and leads me to the third point.

3. Get somebody to help you push.

Going it alone is overrated. We can all benefit from a team. Who's got your back? Who can you trust to help you move forward? And just as importantly, who in your life encourages you to stay stuck? You need less of them and more of the people who see your vision and will say and do things to help you move in the right direction. So let's say you're stuck trying to get your exercise habit going. Team up with a friend who'll help you stay consistent and motivated. Do you find yourself in a financial rut, shopping and charging it all when you can't pay for it? Then stop hanging out with your shopaholic friend. Choose your "push partner" wisely.

My Challenge to You

Push through to your breakthrough.

Coach Yourself

Who or what would most help you push through something difficult right now?

What bold decision is it time to make?

*Be strong and courageous. Do not be afraid;
do not be discouraged, for the* LORD *your
God will be with you wherever you go.*

JOSHUA 1:9

Point to Ponder:

*Decisiveness contributes to your mental and emotional well-
being by creating feelings of happiness and peace.*

A real sign of spiritual and emotional growth occurs when you
stop making decisions based on everyone else's expectations. You end
unhealthy relationships, take a leap of faith toward a new career path,
or speak up for what is right. Some decisions in life are tough. Some
conversations are uncomfortable. Some choices will not be popular.
And yet there are moments when you are called to go against popular opinion and stand apart from the crowd. When you lay your head
down at night, there is no better feeling than that of being at peace
with God. If you must compromise that peace in order to please others, you've compromised everything. Don't do it.

Be bold and courageous in your decisions. Pray. Listen. Don't over-
analyze. Don't "super-spiritualize" it either: Sometimes we pray for
an answer, and when the answer comes through a person or event or
opportunity, we don't recognize it because it's not a booming voice
coming down from heaven. Use your common sense, which is a blessing from God that will help you make the right choice. As a friend
once told me as I agonized over making a change, "You're like the frog
in a pot of cool water who didn't notice that the heat had been turned

up and the water was starting to boil. All he had to do was jump out of the pot!"

Don't worry about what others think. Do what you know is right. No one else has to live your life—or your consequences.

My Challenge to You

Rather than people-pleasing, be bold and courageous in your decisions.

Coach Yourself

What decision are you hesitating over? Who are you trying to please? In your current situation, what would a bold and courageous decision look like?

_____

_____

_____

_____

_____

_____

_____

_____

What one change would make you more productive today?

We are what we repeatedly do.

ARISTOTLE

Point to Ponder:

Americans work more hours per year than any other Western country, taking an average of just 30 days a year of vacation. Europeans, on the other hand, average five to six weeks of vacation time every year.

If you're like most people, items on your to-do list rarely get checked off. Whether you're a procrastinator or just have way too much on your plate—or both—here are some simple ways to be more productive and less stressed:

1. Stop so you can catch up.

It is nearly impossible to focus on current projects when you've got a string of half-finished projects hanging over your head. If you're totally overwhelmed, schedule a block of time to catch up. Don't put anything new on your to-do list; just tackle the loose ends that are draining your energy.

2. Hurrying up slows you down.

How many times have you rushed to do something only to miss a minor detail that caused a major problem? I once went to the wrong airport because in my rush to get out the door, I didn't check that "minor" detail—I was supposed to be at

Washington Reagan Airport. I didn't catch my mistake until I was at the kiosk trying to check in at Baltimore–Washington Airport! Slow down. In the long run, it will save you time and energy.

3. Do the hard stuff first.

It's human nature to put off the hard stuff until later. But when it comes to productivity, tackling the tougher project will give you a sense of accomplishment and you'll waste less time procrastinating. So take a look at your to-do list today, and get busy with the project you keep pushing further down your list.

4. Work in chunks.

Rather than working in really long stretches of time, break your tasks into smaller pieces and give yourself a break as you make progress.

5. Shorten your to-do list.

It's okay to drop some things off of your to-do list altogether. Ask yourself, "Is this essential? Is it a priority?" If not, drop it. If it is essential, but *you* are not essential to getting it done, delegate it.

6. Work less, not more.

The most productive people don't have to stay at the office until 9 p.m. every night. In fact, when you set boundaries around your work hours you'll be more conscious of the need to use your time wisely.

7. Shut out the distractions.

What throws you off track? Chatty coworkers? That chime that lures you back into your e-mail just as you get focused? Solitaire? Whatever it is, find a way to eliminate the distraction during your most focused times. Mute your computer so you don't hear the chime. Uninstall those addictive computer games if you don't have the willpower to resist them. Close your office door, if you have one.

8. Tell someone what you're going to do.

Accountability is a great motivator. Tell someone you trust about your goal to be more productive. Then tell them exactly what you are going to do today. Check in with them at the end of the day.

9. Promise little, if anything at all!

Stop making promises about what you are going to deliver. When you must make a promise, give yourself more time than you think you will need. Instead of, "I'll get that to you by Thursday," say, "I should be able to have that done by Monday morning." When you give it to them on Thursday afternoon or even Friday, you're a star! But if you promise Thursday, and deliver on Friday, not only might someone else be irritated with you, you will probably be irritated with yourself.

10. Have something to look forward to.

When you work hard, play hard. Besides, positive emotion has an added benefit: It helps you deal with stress and adversity better. If you've had a long week at work, get out of the city or take a long walk in the park on the weekend. If you've just completed a major project, schedule time to relax and reconnect with your family. The more you have on your plate, the more important it is for you to take time to enjoy life!

My Challenge to You

Take action to be more productive.

Coach Yourself

Which of these ten productivity principles do you most need to implement in your life right now? When will you begin putting that principle to work?

_____

_____

_____

_____

_____

_____

_____

_____

_____

_____

_____

_____

What's your holding pattern protecting you from?

Delay does not mean denial. Refuse to become anxious because your goal takes longer than you'd like.

Valorie Burton

Point to Ponder:

The ability to wait—or delay gratification— can be a predictor of success.

While I was returning from a speaking engagement on an evening flight, the pilot announced that he expected we would land a few minutes early. Instead, as we approached, nearby thunderstorms changed the plan. We circled for more than an hour, watching daylight turn to evening. At first I found myself—like many of the passengers—feeling agitated. Then I took a deep breath, closed my eyes, and enjoyed a few moments of rest.

I've noticed that so often in life when we encounter a holding pattern, the natural reaction is one of frustration for having to wait. But a holding pattern serves a greater purpose—protecting you until the right conditions unfold that allow you to arrive at your destination safely. In our fast-paced world, we are tempted to believe that faster is always better. Sometimes, though, pushing for something to happen in the wrong timing can unnecessarily force you into a storm.

Today, I invite you to consider an area of your life in which you feel as though you are in a holding pattern. It could be a relationship, your finances, career, or health. Perhaps it's time to relax and practice patience while you wait. Waiting may be your gift in disguise. Take a deep breath, trust God's timing, and calmly embrace the journey.

My Challenge to You

Practice patience and seek rest.

Coach Yourself

In what area of your life do you find yourself in a holding pattern? Is your approach causing you frustration? What shift could you make to alleviate your stress while you wait?

Is your busyness based in fear?

Busyness can serve as a distraction from our reality,
including unfulfilling circumstances
or broken relationships.

Valorie Burton

Point to Ponder:

When you say yes *to things that are not*
purposeful for you, you are essentially
saying no *to your real priorities.*

What is it about saying *no* that makes some of us so anxious? Many people overload their schedules simply because they are too concerned with what others think. Saying no is simple, really: "No, that really doesn't work with my schedule right now." "No, my time with family is so precious, I really can't afford to add another responsibility right now." "No, I have too much else on my plate to give that the attention it deserves." Busyness is often based in fear, and fear of what others might think tops the list.

A friend shared recently that she'd been asked to take on a volunteer project that she wishes she'd never been asked to do. She feels bad about not taking it on so she's trying to figure out how to pile it on top of all of the other stuff on her schedule, including the start of a new school year for her kids, volunteer work at church, and new responsibilities at work. "Well, they really want me to do it and I'd be letting them down if I tried to pass it off to someone else," she explained. "It's just once a week. It's for a good cause." It sounded like she was trying to convince herself rather than me. "What do you think?" she asked.

"I think you should take a deep breath and ask yourself what *you* think," was my response. "What do you sense in your spirit is the right answer?"

"I don't want to do it but I'm worried about what they will think," she replied.

That was the truth. And hearing herself say the obvious gave her the clarity to make a tough decision. The truth will make you free, but first you have to admit it. She found someone to take her place who was enthusiastic about the project and suited to the task.

Taming your hectic schedule is often as easy as learning to say *no* more often. If your life sometimes feels overloaded, I challenge you to get honest with yourself when you feel anxious about a choice you need to make. Consider a decision, a choice, or situation in which you feel anxious about saying *no* even though saying *yes* will result in filling your schedule with an activity that really isn't a priority for you right now. Coach yourself with these questions:

1. **What do you really want to say in this situation?**

   One of the most disarming ways to say no is to tell the person how anxious you feel about saying it. It goes something like this: "I have been really wrestling with telling you this because I'd really like to help, but I just can't. I'm not sure if you'll even understand, but I really hope you will. With all that's on my plate right now, I really can't add anything else."

2. **What are you worried will happen if you say no?**

   In the moment it bombards you, confront your negative thinking. Your imagination can get the best of you when fear is involved. You might tell yourself, "She'll never talk to me again," when the reality is that she'll get over it by tomorrow. And even if she doesn't, you really need to question the health of any relationship in which you cannot be honest without dire consequences.

3. If you say yes, what priorities or goals will get less of your time?

Be realistic. You can't do everything, and adding another ball to the many you're already juggling means one will have to fall. Are you willing to sacrifice time with your family to take on that new project? Are you willing to do a less-than-stellar job on that project at work in order to chair an event?

4. What lesson is this situation offering you right now? Will you embrace the lesson?

Be simple, direct, and honest. Courage is a muscle, and *no* is a word that will help you strengthen it.

When you learn to speak the truth without beating around the bush, you free yourself to focus on your priorities.

My Challenge to You

Refuse to allow fear to overload your schedule.

Coach Yourself

In what way has fear led you to say *yes* to things you really want to say *no* to?

_____

_____

_____

_____

_____

In what way do you need to speak up?

You gain strength, courage, and confidence by every experience in which you really stop to look fear in the face. You must do the thing which you think you cannot do.

ELEANOR ROOSEVELT

Point to Ponder:

One of the most common traits of effective leaders is their ability to effectively communicate in any situation.

While interning for a minor league sports team during graduate school, I heard rumblings one afternoon that civil rights icon Rosa Parks was in the building. Our offices were in the civic center, and she was coming through Tallahassee for a brief appearance. The head coach, a Canadian man who had been alive when Mrs. Parks defiantly—and famously—spoke up for her rights on a city bus in 1955, was determined to see her.

"I'm going to see if I can meet her," he exclaimed, and headed out the door.

I remember thinking, "I want to go too! But who am I? I'm just an intern—a 21-year-old student. I don't want to bother the coach with this. I would love to meet Mrs. Parks, but I don't want to bother her, either. I'm sure she doesn't have time to stop and talk to random strangers."

About 45 minutes later, the coach excitedly and proudly walked back into the office. "I met her!" he said. "And got a photo too." Then he looked at me. "You should have come with me." My heart sank. *What was I thinking?* I thought. If only I'd spoken up. There isn't much I regret in my life, but this moment is one.

I challenge you to speak up. Too often, we bury our voices out of fear—irrational fear about what we have the right to ask for, what others will think, or how they will respond. Whether you need to speak up by asking for what you want, defending something you believe in, or expressing your feelings, know that speaking up is about honoring what you know to be true for you. It's the reason I wrote the book *Why Not You?*—to help you raise your awareness of the ways in which doubt causes you to hesitate so that you can be intentional about defeating it.

The longer you bury your own voice, the more frustrated and angry you become. Are there areas in your life in which you've been silent too long? If so, how could you respectfully and authentically allow your voice to emerge? Whether speaking up means asking for help or letting someone know a boundary has been crossed, seize the moment to let your voice be heard.

My Challenge to You

Speak up! Just say it.

Coach Yourself

In what areas of your life have you been burying your voice or not speaking up when you want to? What do you need to say? When is the best time to say it? What action will you take this week?

Coaching Toolkit

When you ask the right questions, you get the right answers. Use these questions to coach yourself in the areas of resilience and emotional and spiritual well-being. You may want to journal about them or work with a friend or coach to explore your answers.

- What are the three most important signs that indicate success in your life?

- What is the most difficult challenge you've *faced* in your life?

- What is the most difficult challenge you've *overcome* in your life?

- What strengths, people, and wisdom empowered you to overcome your most difficult challenge?

- What is the most persistent doubt that saps your confidence?

- When you consider this most persistent doubt, what empowering truth could you replace it with?

- What is your biggest challenge right now?

- Do you give yourself permission to feel sad, angry, or disappointed, or do you tend to stuff down unwanted emotions?

- Who can you count on when you need encouragement?

- What brings you joy?

- The last time you climbed your way out of a bad mood, what actions did you take to change your attitude?

- What are you most grateful for in your life?

- What accomplishment are you most proud of in your life and what character traits did you call on to accomplish it?

- If God could coach you on your biggest challenge or opportunity right now, what is the first thing you imagine He would say to you?

- What is the thing on your mind that you keep to yourself or tiptoe around—the thing you're not saying?

- When it comes to the thing you're not saying, what do you want to see happen?

- Think back to a time or an event where you felt confident. What gave you that sense of confidence? Is it possible to replicate those circumstances in some way?

- In what ways do you most need to grow spiritually?

- What issues have you stuck in anger, unforgiveness, or hurt? Are you willing to seek professional counseling to work through those issues?

- In what way are you resisting change and what would it look like if you went with the flow?

- In what way is it time for you to speak up?

- What have you been most angry or frustrated with God about? Have you been honest in your prayers about it?

- If you could have a face-to-face conversation with God right now, what three questions would you most like Him to answer? Have you asked those questions in prayer?

- What is it time to bounce back from?

- What is the single most important question you have learned from life's obstacles so far?

Part 2
Business, Career, and Personal Finance

You can only become truly accomplished at something you love. Don't make money your goal. Instead, pursue the things you love doing, and then do them so well that people can't take their eyes off you.

Maya Angelou

Did You Know?

"People with Career Wellbeing are more than twice *as likely to be thriving in their lives overall."*

Tom Rath and Jim Harter[1]

Do you enjoy what you do every day? It's a simple question, but far more significant than you might think. As human beings, we *need* something to do every day. It is a basic element of your overall wellness. Research shows that your daily work—whether paid or unpaid—is a significant predictor of overall mental and physical health. Boredom and lack of daily social contact can be detrimental to your well-being

---

[1] Tom Rath and Jim Harter, *Wellbeing: The Five Essential Elements* (New York: Gallup Press, 2010), 16.

and even lead to depression. The idea of a traditional retirement in which you kick up your feet and do nothing for the rest of your days may sound like a dream in theory, but in reality may not be very realistic—or healthy, for that matter. A classic study of aging men by the late George Gallup showed that those who lived to age 95 didn't retire, on average, until they were at least 80 years old! An overwhelming majority (93 percent) of these men said they got significant satisfaction from the work they engaged in. So if you want to live longer, think not only about putting yourself into a financial position to retire, but think about what you want to do every day once you get there.

You need something that makes you want to get out of bed every morning and embrace the day ahead. This "career" is a part of your identity and it takes up the largest percentage of your time. Even if what you do every day is not a traditional job, you still have a "work" life. If your primary focus is family, that's your work. Why would you spend your time every day doing something you are not called to do or don't like to do?

"Thank God it's Friday" is a mantra so common it is often accepted as normal. But let's just agree that it is *not* normal and it is *not* okay to go through life spending between a third to half of your waking hours doing something that drains you. We were not made to dread work. This section of the book is about finding ways to boost your joy on the job or in your business. For some people that will mean making a tweak here or there—a small change in your habits or the way you go about your business. For others, it will mean a whole transformation in your work life. This section also includes coaching questions about your finances. Since work is the primary way most of us earn an income and you need to be savvy enough with your money habits to eventually retire, it seems appropriate to touch a bit on that subject here.

Your Career and Money Checklist

So just how are you doing when it comes to your work life? Check off only the statements below that hold true for you today:

- [ ] I like what I do every day.

- [ ] When I consider what I will be doing at work on any given day, I am excited to get out of bed in the morning.

- [ ] I enjoy the people I work with.

- [ ] I consider my boss competent.

- [ ] I feel the work I do matters.

- [ ] I have a financial plan for retirement and I am on track with it.

- [ ] I am never bored at work.

- [ ] I often feel in "flow" at work—I am so engaged that I lose track of time.

- [ ] If I want to move up in my company, I have a clear path to advancement.

- [ ] If given the opportunity, I love to learn about ways to be better at what I do.

- [ ] At work, I get to do what I do best by using my gifts and strengths daily.

- [ ] I get regular feedback from my boss or clients that lets me know if I am doing a good job.

☐ My work environment is pleasant.

☐ The compensation or reward I receive for my work feels appropriate to me.

☐ I am not overwhelmed by my work.

☐ I take regular breaks and vacations.

☐ If I were downsized or lost business, I have opportunities beyond my current employer or clients that would allow me to replace my income.

☐ I spend my money in a way that is wise and intentional, not haphazard or emotional.

☐ I have a mentor or coach to answer questions and help me brainstorm about my career goals and options.

☐ I am satisfied that the level of education I currently have will support my highest career goals.

☐ There is no other work I'd rather be doing than the work I am doing now.

____ Total

Are you equipped to handle change at work?

Courage doesn't always roar. Sometimes courage is the little voice at the end of the day that says I'll try again tomorrow.

MARY ANNE RADMACHER

Point to Ponder:

Resilience is the ability to effectively navigate the inevitable changes and setbacks of life. Increasingly, those who are most successful professionally are those who are most resilient in the face of an ever-changing workplace.

Are you one of the millions of people working for an organization that has restructured, changed the rules, or instituted pay cuts to stay afloat in recent years? If so, you're not alone. Dealing with change in the workplace can mean uncertainty and pessimism, neither of which is good for your productivity or stress level. So how do you remain optimistic at work in the midst of crippling uncertainty? Consider these five strategies to navigate unexpected change in the workplace:

1. Choose an attitude of gratitude.

Every day, choose to be grateful for your job. While the job numbers have improved, don't forget that there are still millions of people out of work who would love to trade places with you. Gratitude changes your perspective and helps you appreciate the good rather than simply taking it for granted.

2. Be sure you understand how your role impacts the success of the company.

You want to both understand and maximize your contribution. See the big picture—not just your job and paycheck, but the purpose behind that job and the impact it has on the ability of the organization to survive and excel. As an employee, don't just ask "What can I get?" but "What can I give?" You can contribute to the organization's success. Choose to be a part of the team.

3. Answer your "What if?" questions.

Much of the anxiety that comes from uncertainty is about "What if?" questions. "What if there are more changes and I get a new boss?" "What if they change my position?" "What if this furlough or pay cut becomes permanent?" Answer your questions. Imagine the scenario and then decide how you would handle it if it comes to pass. Doing this exercise can help you see that even if your worst fears become reality, you will find a way to deal with it. You may not like it, but the world will not come to an end. Don't let the anxiety of what *might* happen paralyze you and prevent you from doing your best with what *is* happening right now.

4. Accept what you can't change and change what you can.

There are many aspects of what happens on the job that you simply have no control over. This comes with the territory when you begin employment at a company. Rather than ruminating over the changes that frustrate you, focus on the things that are within your control. This may mean you embrace a new job responsibility with gusto, learn a new skill, or simply adjust your attitude to become more of a team player.

5. Ask, "What is the most important thing I can do right now to secure my future?"

Anxiety is usually about a fear of danger or something we feel we won't be able to handle in the future. Get clear about what that fear is and start addressing it directly. Are you afraid of losing your job because you don't have an emergency cushion? Make it a goal to start building one. Are you anxious that you don't have the connections to land a new job if you lose this one? Make it a goal to start building a strong personal network. Anxious that your skills aren't up-to-date? Make a concerted effort to update your skills and make yourself a more valuable employee. In today's economy, you have to take responsibility and take control of your future. It's not difficult and you're perfectly capable of doing it, but it is a choice.

My Challenge to You

Make peace with uncertainty. Trust that if you face a professional setback or challenge, you are resilient enough to bounce back and move forward.

Coach Yourself

Answer your "What if?" questions. What if the thing you fear most comes to pass? How would you handle it? What would you do? In what ways could you be better because of the experience? Lastly, what step could you take now to make yourself less vulnerable to change and uncertainty?

How strong is your professional network?

More business decisions occur over lunch and dinner than at any other time, yet no MBA courses are given on the subject.

PETER DRUCKER

Point to Ponder:

Research shows that people with a best friend at work are better with customers, produce a better quality of work, are less likely to get hurt on the job, and are seven times more likely to be engaged in their jobs.

Are you starting over in a new career field or perhaps considering a transition? Or have you simply never embraced networking as a part of your career strategy? Whatever the case, strengthening your professional connections is a key to success in the work world—whether you work in corporate America or as a schoolteacher or a healthcare worker. Use these five strategies to build your network or strengthen your existing one.

1. Identify your "why."

Why are you ready to expand your network? What's your goal? Perhaps you are planning a career transition and want to make contacts in a new field to get advice and, eventually, a new job. Maybe you want to gain a new perspective outside your own company. Or perhaps you are just looking to make new friends in a new city, and what better place to start than with people whose career paths mirror your own? Knowing your "why"—or the purpose behind your efforts—will help you narrow and focus your activities.

2. Go where your target audience is.

You need to ask yourself two important questions: What types of people do you most want to connect with? Where do they congregate? Whether it is a professional association, social events, sports activities, or the company gym, go where you will be around the people you'd like to connect with.

3. Ask around!

This is such a simple step, but so many people miss it. Even if it is small, you already have a social and professional circle. Tap into that existing network to ask what you can do to connect with influencers and build your network. What organizations and activities are they connected to? Is there anyone they are willing to introduce you to? Are there events or activities or conferences they could invite you to? Don't be shy. Ask for help.

4. Focus on connecting, not getting.

Get involved with a project or volunteer activity. If you join a group or association, ask, "What can I give?" not just, "What can I get?" When you are willing to get involved in a tangible way, you have an opportunity to actually connect and work with people on the things that matter to you both. It gives you a chance to get to know them beyond a business card or an elevator speech. It also gives them an opportunity to know and observe you. Your work ethic, timeliness, and communication will demonstrate your capabilities and potentially open more doors.

5. Get organized so you can stay in touch.

It is not particularly effective to meet lots of people and not have a strategy to stay in touch. Create your own personal database and schedule regular outreach. For example, every Tuesday you might write personal notes and once a month you might check in via e-mail. Use social networking to build your connections too. LinkedIn and Facebook, for example, can be great tools for connecting and sharing useful information with your newfound connections.

My Challenge to You

Make a decision this week to intentionally build or expand your personal network. Include more people who can support you in living with purpose.

Coach Yourself

What is your vision? What types of people would you like to connect with as you move toward that vision? What steps could you take to expand your network and genuinely connect with such people?

If you'd known then what you know now, what would you have done differently?

I think everyone should experience defeat at least once during their career. You learn a lot from it.

Jim Rohn

Point to Ponder:

One key ingredient to successfully navigating chronic stress is self-efficacy, the belief that you effectively solve problems when they come up.

Everyone has mistakes in their past and episodes they'd rather forget. We wish we could forget those poor decisions and embarrassing moments—but as the old adage goes, if we forget our past we are doomed to repeat it. I challenge you to look back on your past, considering the actions or decisions you wish you could change. What lessons can you take from those experiences?

Here are five pearls of wisdom that will help you embrace your vision for the future instead of staying mired in the past.

1. Go for what you really want.

Don't downsize your dream before you've even attempted it. Go directly for the type of job you want while simultaneously being flexible. Even in a challenging job market, it is not impossible. Remember the guidance to "Shoot for the moon. Even if you miss, you'll land among stars." It applies here. Don't allow fear to keep you from going after what you really want.

2. Place is more important than position.

Landing a job in your field sometimes means landing a job that is beneath your skill level. But if that job puts you in the right environment, you can make connections and be ready when the right opportunity opens up. Salary shouldn't be your only consideration—don't take a job solely because it pays more. Be willing to pay your dues by getting your foot in the door, then show your employer your energy, dedication, and ability. You may get an opportunity to move up once you've proven yourself.

3. No one owes you anything.

One of the biggest complaints I hear from leaders in today's organizations is that too many young people have a sense of entitlement. Experience is a great teacher. Soak up all the knowledge you can. Get a mentor. Listen more than you speak. Don't expect a promotion or raise because you show up and do your job. That's what you're paid to do. Employers don't owe you appreciation, more money, or a bigger job title.

4. Build a foundation for where you want to be ten years from now.

Have a plan for where you want to be in five years or ten years. As I once heard Pastor Dennis Rouse say, if you're not living your vision, you're probably living someone else's. Cultivate a vision for where you want to go. That way you won't wander aimlessly in your career only to find yourself frustrated later because you didn't aim high enough.

5. Build a life, not just a career.

Work hard, yes, but also play hard. As you make plans for the future, think about what you want for your personal as well as your professional life. Don't live to work, *work to live.* When you consider jobs, think about the lifestyle you want to lead. Do you want to be on call 24-7? Do you want to live near family or do you really not mind moving across the country or around the world? Are you willing to live far away for a few years, but plan to move back to your current area? Will your job give you time for a life outside of work?

My Challenge to You

Whether a recent graduate or thirty years out of college, have a clear vision for where you want to be in five or ten years. Start working to make that vision a reality!

Coach Yourself

What are the most important pieces of wisdom you've gleaned in your life, whether from wise teachers or from mistakes you've made (or seen others make)? Knowing what you know now, what advice would you give to someone younger?

_____

_____

_____

_____

_____

_____

_____

_____

What is it time for you to learn?

*The beautiful thing about learning is that
no one can take it away from you.*

B.B. KING

Point to Ponder:

*Lawrence C. Katz, a professor of neurobiology at
Duke University, says brain fitness is as essential as
physical fitness. Whenever you learn a new skill,
you stimulate your brain.*

Every spring, thousands of proud parents watch as their child dons a cap and gown and walks across a stage to earn their diploma or degree. A few years ago, I had the opposite experience. It's not too often that a daughter gets to watch her parent walk across the stage, but I had such a privilege. I was the proud daughter who watched as my father accepted his diploma. He'd spent the previous year earning a master's degree—something he's wanted to do for some time. One of my signature strengths is a love of learning, and perhaps it's a trait I inherited from him.

I want to encourage you to keep learning. You might not want to go back to college to earn a degree, but I'd bet there is something you've been curious about. Whether it's learning to play golf or cook a gourmet meal, picking up a new skill at work or venturing into a whole new career path, it's never too late to learn something new. Learning new things enriches your life, gives you new experiences, and research shows it also strengthens your brain—making your later years more productive and enjoyable.

It can be easy to get stuck in a rut of believing that this is all there is to your life. But the opportunity to learn means the opportunity to grow—to become more than you've previously been. So shake things up a bit. Do something you haven't done before. Pursue a long-held dream. Get outside your comfort zone. Keep on learning!

My Challenge to You

Make a commitment to learn something new.

Coach Yourself

What is it time for you to learn? What have you been curious about? When will you start?

_____

_____

_____

_____

_____

_____

_____

_____

_____

Could your layoff be an opportunity in disguise?

The pessimist sees difficulty in every opportunity.
The optimist sees the opportunity in every difficulty.
WINSTON CHURCHILL

Point to Ponder:

Pessimism can lead to depression. Be careful what
you say to yourself about your circumstances.

Few people *want* to be laid off. But millions have had the experience—and even more know someone close to them who has lost their job. Unemployment is tough, but one key to work through it is optimism. Looking on the bright side can give you the positive energy and the attitude to deal with the not-so-bright side of your situation. While the loss of income and daily connection with coworkers are the most significant factors laid-off workers contend with, there are some surprising ways a layoff can actually make your life better—at least for now:

1. Give me a break!

For most people, there are few times before you retire when you won't have regular work. Rather than looking at it as a loss, embrace this opportunity as a chance to breathe. Although you need to use much of the time for your job search, be sure to take advantage of the opportunity to spend some time resting, being with friends and loved ones, and catching up on projects you've been procrastinating on.

2. Reevaluate your goals.

There's nothing like a pink slip to help you suddenly see your life more clearly. During this time, ask yourself what you *really* want. Consider your personal and professional goals, write them down, and make a plan to reach them. In the daily grind of work and life, such a simple task often gets overlooked.

3. You didn't like that job anyway.

About a third of American workers say they don't enjoy their jobs. Were you one of them? If so, be thankful that you now have a chance to get a job you actually want to go to every day.

4. It's a chance to make a career change.

Perhaps you've been thinking about it for some time. There's another career path you'd like to pursue, but the idea of quitting your job seemed daunting. Things happen for a reason. Perhaps this is serendipity forcing you in the direction you wanted to go anyway.

5. It's a chance to start a business.

Many businesses were started when the owners lost their day jobs. Maybe now is the time for you to put your skills to use as a business owner or consultant. Go for it!

6. It's a chance for more quality time with the people you love.

Rather than moping because you lost your job, find creative and inexpensive ways to have fun with the people you care about. Among people whose incomes have declined during the recession, one common theme is that families began spending more time at home together. With less money for shopping, dining out, and vacations, home-cooked meals and game night with the family became the activities of choice.

7. **It's a chance to see how much less you actually need to be happy.**

When you have less, you often realize you didn't need as much as you thought you did. Use this time to practice the mantra *less is more.* It is.

My Challenge to You

If you are dealing with a layoff or downsizing, seize the opportunity to use the situation to your advantage in some way.

Coach Yourself

What opportunity does this layoff give you? How could you best take advantage of that opportunity?

Is working from home stressing you out?

Our business in life is not to get ahead of others,
but to get ahead of ourselves.

ZIG ZIGLAR

Point to Ponder:

Happy people are productive people.
They do more in a day than others.

Are you one of the 11 million American employees and business owners who work exclusively from home—or do you hope to be? Or, like the 20 million people who work from home at least once a week, does your personal space occasionally become your office? While there are many advantages to working from home, you've probably discovered that it also comes with challenges. Here are five important guidelines for working from home happily and successfully:

1. Set boundaries around your work and family.

Set up your own personal rules. For example, let friends and family know that just because you're at home during the day doesn't mean you can chat on the phone anytime or behave as though every day is Saturday. Agree as a family that they will keep noise down at certain times, minimize interruptions when you are working on an important project, and not play video games on your work laptop.

2. Keep regular hours and close up shop in a visible way.

When work is at home, it is *always* there. You may be tempted to run back to your desk right before bed to read your e-mail or check the status of a project. You're only going to take a minute to do it, but before you know it an hour has passed. Set work hours just as you would if you were going to an office building every day. Set a chime on your phone to remind you when the workday is over. If you have an office, close the door. If your space is more open, get a partition or some other visible means of closing off your work from your home. And unless you are a *very* focused and disciplined person, don't attempt to work and do laundry or listen to the television or anything else you wouldn't normally do at work in a commercial or corporate space.

3. Don't let work take over the house.

If you have your laptop on the nightstand, bedroom slippers in your office, or fax machine in the kitchen, you know what I'm talking about. Do your best to keep your home environment free of work reminders. When you work outside the house, it can be easier to make your home a sanctuary from stress and deadlines. When you work from home, making home a sanctuary is a challenge. If you have the luxury of a separate room for an office, choose a room away from your bedroom if possible. And if you have to squeeze your workspace into a more confined living space, do your best to set it up anywhere but the bedroom. The bedroom is a sanctuary within your sanctuary. Guard it fiercely!

4. Leave the house from time to time.

Every once in a while you might get a little stir-crazy working at home. While most workers complain about the commute, at-home workers sometimes crave one—a commute somewhere, anywhere! Starbucks. The post office. FedEx! If you don't have a lot of outside meetings, schedule time away from the house a couple times a week, taking your work to a library or coffee shop where you can still focus on the tasks at hand.

5. Reach out.

One of the most devastating effects of a layoff is a lack of social connection—an issue that affects millions of solopreneurs and telecommuters who feel isolated from people. Join or form a group of like-minded professionals and communicate frequently. Make an effort to meet others for breakfast or lunch instead of communicating in a phone meeting. According to researchers at Gallup, we all need about six hours of social time each day (including e-mail and phone calls) to maximize our well-being. Since you're not sitting in an office building surrounded by people, you'll have to be even more intentional about connecting with others.

My Challenge to You

Notice how working from home impacts your personal life and make a decision to minimize any stressful effects.

Coach Yourself

What aspect of working from home causes stress for you or members of your family? What could you do to alleviate or minimize that stress?

Are you a communication leader at work?

The trouble with talking too fast is you may say something you haven't thought of yet.

ANN LANDERS

Point to Ponder:

Good communication can cut down on frustration and inefficiencies that lead to more work.

If you're like so many people in today's world, you have a *lot* on your plate. And too much busyness can mean unnecessary mistakes, misunderstandings, and tension on the job that just makes the stress worse. So how can you learn to communicate better, even when it feels like you are too busy to slow down?

When you're overwhelmed and overloaded, it can sometimes be tempting to bypass communication altogether. You don't take time to make that quick phone call, shoot off an e-mail, or hold an impromptu meeting to make sure everyone is on the same page. *This is a big mistake.* Resilient workers know that good communication up front is one of the keys to successfully managing an overloaded schedule. There is nothing worse than thinking something is checked off your to-do list only to have it come back around again because it wasn't right the first time. If you don't want to double up on work and waste time fixing preventable mistakes, make communication a top priority. Coach yourself with these five questions:

1. Last time I had to put out a fire or fix a mistake, what conversation could have prevented it from happening?

Think about the last time you were frustrated over having to redo something. If you'd taken that one extra step to clarify or make a phone call to verify information or confirm a detail with someone, there is a good chance the mistake could have been avoided. Take a lesson from the mistakes that have happened so you don't keep repeating them. Notice your patterns and make some new, simple rules that will save you time even though it will take a little extra time.

2. **If you don't communicate about the matter at hand, will the consequences matter a month from now?**

A lot of people are swamped because they communicate *too much*. They fight every battle—and the truth is, every battle doesn't have consequences worth worrying about. And when you overcommunicate, the real priorities get lost. People tend to pay less attention to all of it. When your time is limited, be selective about what you communicate. This way you will save your time and energy, and what you say will have a greater impact on the people you say it to.

3. **Every time you communicate at work, ask, "What's the outcome I'm looking for?"**

Always begin with the end in mind, especially when your time is limited. Don't walk away from a conversation or an e-mail exchange without the information or outcome you need to move forward. Otherwise, you'll need to revisit it later—and you've already established that you don't have time to do that. You shouldn't leave a conversation feeling *more* confused than before you had it.

4. **Am I avoiding the conversation or am I avoiding the person?**

Let's face it. Sometimes we avoid communication because we want to avoid the person we need to communicate with. But their drama doesn't have to become our drama. Rather than getting sucked into emotions, slights, and even other people's stress, take a deep breath and focus on the content, not the emotion. Remember, you don't have time to fight every battle. Keep your eye on the task at hand, but don't let fear keep you from gathering or sharing the information you need to keep moving forward on your job.

5. Is e-mail really the best way to communicate that message? Or would another mode of communication be more effective?

We've all received an e-mail and thought, "What the heck did he mean by that?" Or perhaps you've sent an e-mail you later regretted. So many of our advances in technology over the last couple of decades have been about communication tools, but not all tools are effective in every work situation. E-mail does not convey tone, and this can create conflict and misunderstanding faster than anything else. Not everyone reads every e-mail. Most of us are buried in e-mail every day. Don't assume someone got your message, and don't use e-mail to communicate something that will negatively impact someone. Pick up the phone or talk to the person face-to-face. If your message is complex or involves a lot of instructions, writing it in an e-mail can be helpful, but follow up with a phone call.

My Challenge to You

Use communication as a tool to take charge rather than create a hindrance to productivity.

Coach Yourself

When was the last time a lack of communication became a stumbling block? What will you do to prevent something like this from occurring again?

Are you really ready for a career change?

Learn to be happy with what you have
while you pursue all that you want.

JIM ROHN

Point to Ponder:

It's worth aiming for a job with a quick and simple
commute. Having one will boost your happiness.

With changes in the economy in recent years, many people have changed careers or are considering it. Others, including Baby Boomers, are interested in making a "late-career" change. This is a big decision, and one that's worth a great deal of thoughtful consideration. So how can you successfully transition into an entirely new career?

Here are five questions to answer *before* you make a career transition:

1. Do I really want a whole new career or just a new situation?

Don't throw the baby out with the bathwater. Think back to a time in your career when you felt enthusiastic about your work. Were you in the same field? What would it take to use more of the strengths and skills you used in that favorable scenario? If you've never been enthusiastic about your work and there is no hope for building on the career you've already established, *then* it's time to look at new options. Have a vision. Write it down.

2. What am I missing in my current career that I want in a new one?

Be very vivid and specific. If it is more income, name the exact number or range you're looking for. If it is the ability to use a particular skill set, be clear about what specific talents and abilities you would like to use every day. If it is time with your family, be specific about how much time and when. Do you want to be home with them in the early afternoons? Have more time to take vacations together as a family? Rate the importance of each item on your list. What things must be in place in order for it to really be worthwhile to abandon your current career? Think about compensation, flexibility, location, types of tasks, emotional satisfaction, opportunity for advancement, and whatever else will indicate to you, "Yes! This move is really worth it."

3. What do I have in my current career that I might have to give up in a new one?

The grass often looks greener on the other side...until you get there. Don't take for granted what you already have. Make a list of what's good about your current career. Rate the importance of each item on this list just like you rated the importance of the things you'll gain in a new career. Do the pros really outweigh the cons? Will what you gain outweigh what you give up?

4. Do I have the "real scoop" on the new career?

It can be easy, especially when frustrated in your current career, to idealize what it will be like to land in a new field. However, your expectations could be dead wrong. The only way to know is to talk to people who are already there. Talk to more than one person—preferably at least three. Have a standard list of questions you want answers to. Ask the same questions of each person so you can get multiple perspectives.

5. Can I leverage my current experience so that I am not starting from scratch?

Ideally, some of your experience and background will be relevant to your new career. If there is any way to make that experience count, do your best to leverage it. If you're finding it difficult to connect the dots between your experience to date and your new career goal, talk to a career coach, mentor, or someone already in the field you aspire to. They may be able to see your experience from a different perspective and give you advice on what aspects of your background to play up as you seek opportunities in your new field.

My Challenge to You

Before you opt for a major transition in your career, stop and ask yourself some tough questions.

Coach Yourself

Is it really a new career you want, or do you need to make some adjustments in your current career?

_____

_____

_____

_____

_____

What's your personal PR strategy?

*Great work is done by people who are
not afraid to be great.*

FERNANDO FLORES

Point to Ponder:

*The quickest way to get noticed is to do such good work that
others can't help but notice it.*

Celebrities and huge companies aren't the only ones who benefit from a good public relations campaign. Smart workers and business owners employ a public relations strategy of their own. Do you have one? Good PR will help you develop and grow relationships, gain more influence on the job, and land on your feet quickly should you ever find yourself out of work. It's not about being a shameless self-promoter, but instead being a proactive manager of your own image. It's about being a communicator people trust. Here are five steps to get you started.

1. All PR is not good PR.

There's a saying that all press is good press, meaning it's better to have people talking about you than not noticing you at all—even if they're saying bad things. This may work for celebrities who get rewarded for bad behavior with book deals and new TV shows, but it rarely works in the real world. Don't be a magnet for drama. If you don't know what you're talking about, stay quiet until you get your facts straight. And know that being self-centered in a work environment that prizes teamwork will not do you any favors. "Me, me, me" doesn't go over well in the business world. Be very intentional about the image you present. Protect it. Polish it. Then, present it.

2. Communicate your wins consistently.

Businesses put out press releases. You should too. Call them memos, e-mails, tweets, whatever. Communicate! Target the audience you most need to reach in order to achieve your goals. In many cases, this means your boss. If you own the business or work with customers, it means your clients and prospects. It isn't about bragging, but communicating consistently. Keep your boss in the loop about where you are on a project. That way, she's not left wondering and can relax knowing you're on top of it. If you have an idea that will save the company time or money, mention it. Better yet, outline how it will save time and money, then present it.

3. Collaborate and celebrate others.

The difference between shameless self-promotion and good PR is the focus on relationships. When you genuinely celebrate the wins of others, you strengthen relationships, build trust, and learn from them as well. Don't go it alone. Instead, build connections that will empower you to reach your goals more quickly and easily than you can alone.

4. Don't tell your business—or anyone else's.

While you want to be intentional about communicating your progress and strong ideas, be quiet when it comes to sharing the details of your personal business or private office matters. Tune in to what's going on around you, but don't get sucked into office gossip or take sides. If you do, you may eventually find yourself on the wrong side. If someone gossips to you about others, you can be pretty sure they will gossip to others about you. Gossip can backfire, so make a decision not to participate.

5. Be kind. Be bold.

Notice I said be *kind*, not nice. Nice is bland. Nice is often not even authentic, and people notice that. Instead, focus on being kind and gracious to people. Tell the truth, but be gentle when you tell it. Being arrogant, disrespectful, or obnoxious may get your point across, but you'll eventually pay the price. It is interesting to note that one of the top strengths of leaders is love and compassion. This may be, in part, because we feel close to and trusting of those with such qualities. To stand out, be bold in your own unique way. While teamwork is essential for success, leaders also know when to take a stand rather than following the crowd. If you do, soon the crowd—and the opportunities—will be following you.

My Challenge to You

Be proactive about managing your image and career.

Coach Yourself

What current career goals would better "personal PR" help you reach? What specifically will you do to improve your outreach and facilitate the achievement of those goals?

_____

_____

_____

_____

_____

In what way do you need to be unconventional?

Life is either a daring adventure or nothing.
HELEN KELLER

Point to Ponder:
The more you come to understand yourself, the more comfortable you are with making bold decisions that are authentic to who you truly are.

Some of the wisest decisions you can make are counterintuitive. In the process of living, it can be easy to do what it seems has always been done—to follow the path well-traveled. But if you stop for a moment and listen to the whispers of your heart's desire, you'll often find that it is the unconventional path that makes the most sense for you.

Now, to be clear, such unconventional moves are not for everyone. After you listen to your heart, you must also use a little logic by following some simple but important rules. Consider these five risky career moves that have been known to pay off. Do any of them resonate with you? If any of them do, prayerfully proceed with courage and a sound plan—and enjoy the journey!

1. **Saying goodbye to your current career and hello to a new one.**
   If you lack passion for your work or don't get to use your strengths, your industry is in decline or opportunities for growth are limited, forging into new career territory could be

a wise decision. But avoid choosing a new career because it's a "hot new career path" when you don't have the strengths or passion for it.

2. Saying no to a promotion.

This unconventional choice can pay off when you are already overwhelmed, or more money or a bigger title won't get you the visibility or skills to achieve your true goals. Saying yes and then doing a poor job can be more detrimental to your career than saying no. Don't allow the "disease to please" to turn you into the person who gets everything dropped on her desk with little appreciation or financial reward.

3. Becoming your own boss.

This is a dream that is both possible and rewarding, but doing it well takes more work than you might think. Plan your transition, ease into full-time entrepreneurship, and prepare financially and personally for the challenges of business ownership. Taking that leap of faith too soon based on excitement for an idea or frustration with a job can be a mistake.

4. Going back to school.

This move makes sense when it will directly impact your ability to reach your career goals, it is required in order to move to the next level, and you can afford it (the financial investment will reap a gain beyond the cost of the education). A common mistake is the belief that a degree is the golden ticket to landing a great new job. Do your homework to find out what's really needed for your ideal job. It might be experience over education—or a different path of education than the one you're considering. If it's a degree, research the school you choose thoroughly to determine their track record for graduate placement in your career of choice.

5. Taking some time off.

A sabbatical. Time to raise your children. A dream lifestyle that allows you to have time for what really matters most. Sounds dreamy, doesn't it? Well, it can be, but it's also a risky move to step out of the workforce or even reduce your schedule to part-time. It can pay off, though, when it meets your family's life goals, you prepare financially, and you find a way to keep some skills current so that you are positioned to reenter the workforce when you are ready. Stay plugged in to your professional connections though. Be strategic about your time off and you will have options when you are ready to go back to work.

My Challenge to You

Be willing to take risks when you sense in your spirit it is the right thing for you to do.

Coach Yourself

Do any of these "risky" career moves make sense for you? If so, which ones? Have you taken one of these moves before? If so, what lessons did you learn that you will carry forward in your future?

What would it take for you to get ahead at work?

Whatever you do, do it heartily, as to the Lord and not to men.

COLOSSIANS 3:23 NKJV

Point to Ponder:

Sleep acts as a daily reset button and clears out stressors from the previous day, enabling you to operate at a higher capacity.

Who gets ahead more in the workplace—is it the in-your-face self-promoter or the modest person who works hard and sometimes lets her accomplishments go under the radar? More importantly, what's your style? And how can you adjust it to get noticed and land that next promotion? Coach yourself with these five questions to start getting noticed by your boss, so you can move to the next level.

1. What are the top five things your boss and company value?

Study your boss and your company culture. Everyone's interests are about what's in it for them. So what's in it for your boss if she promotes you? How do you make your boss's job easier? How do you make her department look better, which in turn makes her look good? What's her style? Does she value proactive employees who come up with ideas, or ones who are great at implementing hers? Does she value timeliness over perfection? Then get it in on time, even if you think it needs a little more polish. Understand what motivates your boss, and you can unlock the key to winning her over.

2. Is it time to adapt your approach?

If your style isn't working for you, change it. So, if your company culture values teamwork and modesty, pull back on the shameless self-promotion. If your company values those who can toot their own horn, start giving a regular account of the results you are delivering. Yes, this may take you out of your comfort zone, but big enough goals always take you out of your comfort zone. Get comfortable with being uncomfortable. The definition of insanity, as we all know, is to keep doing the same thing over and over and expect different results.

3. What's the most persistent but solvable problem you have the power to fix?

Maximize your role in your current position. Rather than focusing on the next job you want, focus on mastering the job you have. Those who get ahead focus on solutions, not problems. See the big picture and know that you can have a role in making that picture better.

4. Are you disciplined?

Research shows that talent is not enough to really make it to the top. It takes consistency in performance, and that takes discipline. Take a look at your last performance review. Think back on the advice or feedback you've gotten over the last year. What is one change you could make consistently that would dramatically improve your performance? This could be as simple as a daily meeting to help you get organized. A new commitment to arriving on time. A decision to learn a new skill. Whatever it is, commit to it and practice it daily. Small, incremental changes often create significant shifts that turn the tide.

5. Are you happy?

This is going to sound counterintuitive, but studies have shown that people with higher levels of positive emotion are more likely to be promoted and get raises. We often think it is success, promotions, and more money that make us happier, but it is actually the other way around. Happiness creates success. So here's a little-known strategy for landing that promotion—start having fun outside work. Choose a positive attitude *at* work. It attracts opportunity.

My Challenge to You

Manage your career by choosing excellence and a strategic approach that will get you noticed.

Coach Yourself

In your role and workplace, what's the most persistent but solvable problem you have the power to fix? What could you do to alleviate that problem for the company?

What's your personal brand?

You can't build a reputation on what you are going to do.
HENRY FORD

Point to Ponder:
*It is easiest to market yourself when you choose to
authentically be yourself.*

Oprah. Martha Stewart. Dr. Phil. Each of them is known for something—and as soon as you hear the name, their powerful personal brand comes to mind. But celebrities and business tycoons aren't the only ones who can benefit from a personal brand. Whether you realize it or not, you have a brand too. When people think of you, an image springs to mind. Maybe it's *creative, efficient,* or *good with numbers.* The question is, is your brand helping you or hurting you? In the workplace, the workers with the most powerful brands are the ones who get ahead. Start crafting your brand intentionally, and you could see your career skyrocket. Take your cues from household names and apply them to your own career. Begin with these five strategies to build a personal brand that will make you stand out from the crowd:

1. Know your "why."

Every strong brand is clear about its mission. Why is the company better off because you work there? Based on your strengths and gifts, get clear about your purpose—your "why." When you think Oprah, you think *Live your best life.* When you think Tyler Perry, you think *Family-friendly black entertainment.* When your boss thinks of you, what do you want to come to mind? Are you a consensus-builder? Out-of-the-box thinker? Expert salesman? The person who can tackle any challenge and win? Get clear about your "why"—your personal mission—and do something daily that embodies it.

2. Take a risk.

A brand is built from scratch. At some point it becomes well known, but that is usually after taking a leap of faith to pursue the dream. Is it time for you to try something new, initiate a career-changing conversation, or step back into the work you really want to be doing? It costs nothing to dream. Go for it.

3. Be the solution to an unsolved problem.

Brands with staying power identify an opportunity and seize it. What challenge or problem is waiting to be solved in your department? Find a way to solve problems that impact morale, customers, and the bottom line. If you do, the company will soon be looking to you as a go-to person. Your career and your income will be better for it.

4. Be consistent.

Make a plan for where you are headed. Then work your plan. Stick with it. The best brands don't change direction with the wind. As a result, they are trusted because people know what to expect. Know your mission. Create a vision. Be consistent in your performance.

5. Be confident in your own personal style.

Successful brands are not bland. They have a unique way of going about things. From taking care to look your best to being intentional about how you treat people, develop a personal style that is memorable and meaningful.

My Challenge to You

Start crafting your own personal brand.

Coach Yourself

Who has your favorite personal brand? What is it that stands out most about that person? What is the most important lesson you can glean from their career? How might you apply that lesson in your own career?

_____

_____

_____

_____

_____

_____

_____

_____

_____

_____

How will you know it's worth going back to school?

If a man empties his purse into his head,
no one can take it from him.
BENJAMIN FRANKLIN

Point to Ponder:

Education can lead to increased opportunities. However,
research shows that there is no correlation between
education and happiness.

With the average in-state college tuition costing over seven hundred dollars per class, going back to school won't be a cheap decision. But more and more people, from twenty-somethings to Baby Boomers, are going back to school in an effort to increase their career opportunities and job security. But how do you determine whether or not it's worth it? Consider these guidelines:

1. You've figured out how to pay for it.

The best option, when at all possible, is to find a way to go to school without ending up in debt. Don't pass up free money: Check into employer tuition assistance programs, grants, and scholarships that may be available. Carefully consider where you will go to school—public, in-state schools typically offer the lowest tuition rates. Also consider working and going to school so you can pay as you go. Going to school should help you increase your income, not put you in a worse bind than where you were prior to going to school. If loans are unavoidable, take a realistic look at how much debt you will incur. How much will those payments be after you finish school?

2. You can make the time commitment.

For students who need flexible scheduling options, this is the best time in history to pursue higher education. Most universities now have options for those who need to go to school at night or on the weekends, or who want to attend classes from home. Online programs at top universities abound. Do your homework! You might be very surprised by the undergraduate majors and graduate programs offered online by major brick-and-mortar universities. Some companies will allow you to adjust your schedule if what you are studying will benefit them. Get your family on board too, so that you can get help with responsibilities that may be harder to keep up with now that you have the added schoolwork.

3. It will give you the lifestyle you want.

Finding a new career option that means fewer hours or more flexibility can prove very meaningful, particularly if you work in a demanding career or field. For example, a television producer who decides to become a dental hygienist so she can have more predictable, less stressful work hours does so to have more time for her family without sacrificing her income. If you are nearing retirement age and want to find a second career that will give you enjoyment and income without a 40-hour work-week, going back to school may also prove to be worthwhile.

4. Education is a longtime dream unfulfilled for you.

Many people fit into this category. They started college, but didn't finish. They always wanted to go to grad school, but life and kids and other things happened, and their educational dreams fell by the wayside. Mark Twain once said, "It isn't the things we did that we most regret, but the ones we didn't do."

If you've always regretted not finishing school and you have career dreams beyond where you are now, make a plan to go back to school so you can realize your potential. Be smart about it, though. Find the options that will work for you financially.

5. You choose the right school and program.

Not all schools and programs are created equal. Research which types of jobs graduates of a program are landing. Consider the reputation of the program. Ask your employer or mentors for recommendations. Look at those who have already achieved what you are aiming for. What programs did they attend? What do they recommend? Be discerning. There are times when it is worth it to pay more for a particular school or program—like when the name of the school alone is likely to open doors for years to come, or when the program has a reputation for placing more students than another program. Also, apply for scholarships and grants, if you are eligible. Don't let free money slip out of your hands.

6. Your career field is in a downward trend.

Going back to school can be a very smart, proactive move— especially if you see that you are in an industry that is in decline. Maybe jobs in your industry are becoming more scarce or more demanding due to downsizing. It's just not what you signed up for. If so, it's time to reinvent yourself. And going back to school can be an effective strategy to reclaim a great career for yourself.

7. More education will lead to a significantly higher salary.

What will be the return on your investment if you go back to school? Education is an investment that can reap rewards for years to come. It can never be taken from you. Do your homework to get clear about how much more you can earn annually as a result of going back to school. Compare that to the cost of going back to school. Also, keep in mind that more education doesn't always mean another degree. There are many certificate programs from very reputable schools that give you the requisite skills to achieve your career and financial goals. If you're going to take out $80,000 in loans, but increase your income by $10,000 per year, it will take eight years to recoup your investment. Is that worth it to you?

My Challenge to You

Be smart about your education. Plan for it before you go for it.

Coach Yourself

Do you have a dream of more formal education? What will you need to do to make that dream a reality?

_____

_____

_____

_____

_____

_____

_____

_____

Are opportunities chasing you down?

Your profession is not what brings home your paycheck.
Your profession is what you were put on earth to do
with such passion and such intensity that it
becomes spiritual in calling.

Vincent van Gogh

Point to Ponder:

Your greatest potential can only be experienced when
you tap into your strengths to meet the challenges
and opportunities before you.

A friend recently mentioned that a very major company was court-ing him for a dream job at a dream salary. What made the conversa-tion so noteworthy was that it was the third time in less than a year that he had called me to coach him through the same dilemma: Was it worth leaving a solid, happy job for the promise of something slightly better? Despite a weaker economy in the last few years, there are still people who are fielding multiple job offers. What are these folks doing differently than others? Most have a powerful personal brand—and you can have that too.

In the rapidly changing marketplace, the rules have changed. Just about everyone is a "free agent," and that means that to move up in the company or to land a position with a new company, you need to man-age yourself like a brand. What are you known for? Why does your employer need *you* rather than the next guy with a similar background and education? Consider these five strategies:

1. Manage your career like a business.

Gone are the days when you could rely on a company to tell you what your career path would be. Today you must be proactive. Have a vision. Set goals. Seek insight and feedback. Keep learning. Market yourself. It's You, Inc.

2. Be known for something.

This "something" adds value and makes you stand out. One woman who ascended the ranks quite early in her career was known for getting things done quickly. As a twenty-something, this became her focus. She was so good at being fast that she documented her process and shared it with executives. They revamped their procedures and saved thousands of dollars as a result. Her "brand" got her noticed and promoted several times. Eventually, being fast was not her focus anymore. By that point, she was where she wanted to be.

3. Be likable.

Of course, everyone won't necessarily like you. But if you're kind, drama-free, and dependable, it will take you a long way.

4. Have an expansive network you intentionally nurture.

Being in demand doesn't just happen. You must work at it. Again, manage your career like a business. Maintain a database of contacts and keep in touch with them. Reach out to them when they need help, and they'll be eager to help you in turn.

5. Be willing to go where the opportunities are.

Those who are getting unsolicited job offers in this market are often getting them from outside their own city. If the opportunity is a smart one, sometimes that means making a move. Sometimes you have to be willing to go where the opportunities are.

My Challenge to You

Set yourself up so that you are in demand.

Coach Yourself

What would lead to better opportunities for you in your line of work? What could you begin doing now that would make you more in demand?

How would it feel to work less?

Work to live. Don't live to work.
VALORIE BURTON

Point to Ponder:
Happier people are more productive, thereby getting more work done in less time than others.

Imagine for a moment what it would feel like to work *less*—if you could focus more on your family and other things that matter in your life. Work is wonderful, especially when you are passionate about it. But there's more to life than work, so what would it be like if you didn't have as much? What would you do with the extra time? Who would you spend it with? Whether you want to reduce your hours at your current job or eventually stop working to focus on your family, consider these four strategies:

1. Restructure your day and break bad work habits.

Are you working too many empty hours? Could a 50-hour workweek really be a 40-hour week? Many workers work hard, but not smart. So working less, if you are in this category, is a matter of breaking some bad work habits. If you are the first one in and the last one out every day, something might be wrong. Create personal deadlines to force yourself out of the office if you need to—for example, schedule a 5:30 dinner date or class at the gym so you must leave the office on time. Find ways to eliminate distractions so you can use your time in the office more efficiently.

2. If you want to work fewer than 40 hours, know your company.

If you want to work fewer than 40 hours you've got to know the culture at your company and prepare accordingly. In some workplaces, working less will mean no or slow promotions. You must decide whether or not you are okay with that. But in today's new economy, there are many businesses that would love to spend less money on employees who can give them a real bang for their buck. In those companies, scaling back is not necessarily a career killer—as long as you make an impact. If you work fewer hours but give your all and make a contribution to the bottom line, you will always be seen as a valuable player. So part of the strategy for working less is being strategic and performing at your best, whether you're working 40 hours a week or 20.

3. Can you afford to work fewer than 40 hours? If so, make a plan.

Ask yourself how you can prepare financially. For most people, one of the main purposes of work is earning a living. The doors open wide to work less when you live below your means. If you quit your job or scaled back on your hours, would you be able to make it? If not, make a plan to get to the point where you don't have to work so much. Know exactly what that number is. Trim your expenses and save, save, save!

4. If you want to work fewer than 40 hours, ask yourself if it is time to switch careers.

This option would be a long-term solution—a higher-paying job down the road for fewer hours than you work now. Ask yourself, "What opportunity would allow me to earn more for my time?" Many people in this economy have been forced to make a transition to new lines of work. One good thing that can come of a forced transition is the opportunity to reevaluate your options. A different career path could dramatically increase your income while demanding less of your time. This option may require time to prepare or train, but can be a smart, long-term solution to the problem of overwork. Especially for those thinking of starting a family who know they don't want a job with long hours as a parent, think ahead and plan for a transition to working less.

My Challenge to You

Dream big. It's possible to work less in your future.

Coach Yourself

What would it look like for you to work less? Does this idea appeal to you? Why or why not? If you'd like to make it happen, what is your vision for it?

How resilient are you?

*Most great people have attained their greatest success
just one step beyond their greatest failure.*

Napoleon Hill

Point to Ponder:

*A strong support system is a key to resilience.
Never underestimate the power of good relationships
to help you through difficult challenges.*

In the face of downsizing, outsourcing, and higher demands on
your productivity, would your employer call you resilient? Resilience
is a skill more and more companies are looking for in their employees—people who can embrace change rather than fight it. Why is it so
timely now and how can you be more resilient at work?

As I speak at major companies around the country, this is a theme
that comes up over and over again. Longstanding, stable companies
are dealing with more change than ever before, and these changes can
be startling to employees. Many are very resistant. The people who
are getting ahead, keeping their jobs, and even fielding multiple job
offers to steal them away, are the ones who understand this and are a
part of the answer companies are looking for to give them an edge in
this economy.

1. Embrace what is.

Your company reality simply may not be what it used to be.
Quit hanging on to what was and embrace what is. This is a
major issue. Companies ask me regularly, "How can we get

people to see the reality? Sales are not what they used to be, customers are not spending like they used to, and competition has crept up on us with changes in technology and customer expectations. We need our employees to change with us if we are going to survive." There's a good chance that this is your company's reality too. Remember, your boss is always keeping an eye on the bottom line.

2. Don't let change intimidate you.

If you work for an employer that's been the same for decades and decades, it can be frightening when they start to make changes. You wonder if your position is secure. You wonder if you can adjust to new ways of doing things. But don't let change scare you. Make a decision to embrace it. Be willing to learn. Having the right attitude can make the difference between moving up and moving out.

3. Be a bridge builder.

Can you be an employee who inspires and gets others on board with the changes and new reality that exists at your company? If so, you're going to be a real asset. Rather than joining in the complaining and resistance, be the person who seeks to understand the reasons behind the change and have a positive impact on coworkers and employees. This doesn't even mean you have to agree with the changes. Simply accept that some things have changed and be willing to do your part to help the company be successful. Understand your company's biggest challenges and be a solution.

4. Don't isolate yourself.

Isolation is a career killer. Relationships are the key to career success. Even if you are in a position—for example, IT—in which you don't have to manage or interact with a lot of people on a daily basis, make it a goal to reach out, keep your boss and coworkers abreast of your progress, and simply be someone others want to be around. When difficult decisions are made, those with strong relationships at work are more likely to weather the storms.

5. Bounce back—over and over again.

Resilient people think differently. They are optimistic in the face of a challenge. So you've got to pay attention to what you're telling yourself about the things going on at work. "I can't do this" and "I don't want to deal with all these changes" must be replaced with thoughts such as, "I've never done this before, but I can learn."

My Challenge to You

Be resilient at work.

Coach Yourself

Would your employer and employees call you resilient? Do you make change easier or harder on yourself and those around you? What would it look like for you to become more resilient?

_____

_____

_____

_____

_____

_____

How are your social media habits influencing your career goals?

You can buy attention (advertising). You can beg for attention from the media (PR). You can bug people one at a time to get attention (sales). Or you can earn attention by creating something interesting and valuable and then publishing it online for free.

DAVID MEERMAN SCOTT

Point to Ponder:

Staying abreast of technology and industry trends can help you appear more knowledgeable and adaptable in a dynamic marketplace.

Many professionals know the obvious when it comes to social media: Don't post questionable photos, don't blast your last employer, don't post anything offensive. Ask yourself, "Would I mind this being broadcast on the news tomorrow?" If the answer is yes, then don't post it! If you wouldn't say it on camera, don't say it online.

But those are the don'ts. What are the do's of social media that will make you look good to an employer and boost your career or business prospects? Do you have a personal online strategy? Consider these five rules to use social media to your career advantage.

1. Use social media as a personal PR tool.

In this new world, *everyone* is a public figure. Manage yourself like one. Decide what you want your image to be and use social media to build that image. Make sure your bio and other descriptions are well-written and connect with your target audience. Social media shows employers at a glance how well you communicate, and research shows that strong communicators are more likely to get promoted and make good leaders.

2. Stay abreast of industry trends and share them.

Share relevant, intriguing articles that are related to your industry and your career goals. This shows an employer you are paying attention to trends. Every post doesn't have to be about the industry, but incorporate it into your online presence.

3. Be intentional about who you let into your network.

When your primary purpose is professional networking, build your network with people you know and trust. Don't feel guilty about ignoring friend requests. If you don't want to let in clients or acquaintances, but only close friends, set your profile to private so that you are not searchable.

4. Manage your photos like a publicist.

Post only pictures that show you in a way you don't mind circulating the Internet. Personal photos are fine, just not compromising ones. Un-tag photos that you don't like and ask friends to remove ones you don't want. If they refuse, un-friend them. Damaging photos can be costly in more ways than one. Once you post them, they are out of your hands. Even if you remove them from your files, others may already have saved them.

5. Think of your social presence like you do a credit report.

A credit report measures risk. Employers use a social media background check in much the same way. It is another measure of whether or not hiring you will pay off. Do you show good judgment? Are you proactive about managing your career? Do you communicate effectively and with discretion?

My Challenge to You

Become social media savvy.

Coach Yourself

When it comes to your use of social media, in what ways do you want your social media presence to enhance your career? List at least two or three specific goals.

_____

_____

_____

_____

_____

_____

_____

_____

_____

Could you turn your passion into profit?

There is no passion to be found in playing small—
in settling for a life that is less than the
one you are capable of living.

Nelson Mandela

Point to Ponder:

Doing work you love has a significant
impact on your well-being.

"Do what you love, Val, and the rewards will come." This was a piece of advice given to me by one of my mentors not long after I first began working. I was intrigued yet skeptical when he said it. If I followed my passion, would the rewards really come? I have since discovered that the answer is *yes*. One of the chapters in my book *Rich Minds, Rich Rewards* is appropriately titled "Do what you love and the rewards will come." The rewards don't always come overnight, but they do come in divine timing. What is it that you'd like to do (or do more of) for a living? The most gratifying rewards are fulfillment and joy, but today I want to share five questions that will help you reap financial rewards while doing work about which you are passionate. Whether you are starting a business, transitioning out of a career for which your passion has dwindled, or seeking that next promotion or job, answer these five questions to help you increase the financial rewards of doing what you love:

1. What difference are you passionate about making in others' lives?

Notice I didn't ask "what are you passionate about"? Instead I want you to determine the purpose of your passion, which is using it to positively impact the world. That type of drive attracts opportunities that often lead to raises, job offers, and new business. To turn your passion into profit, you must fulfill a purpose that others need or want. Unfortunately, people and companies aren't particularly concerned with whether or not you get to pursue your passion. They spend money on people, products, and services that fulfill their needs and desires. When you find a way to allow your passion to make a positive and needed impact on others, you have a winning formula!

2. Have you mastered your craft?

It isn't enough to have talent. Allow your passion to fuel a desire to learn more about your field of endeavor and improve your skills and knowledge. Those who master their craft go above and beyond others in their field. They introduce new ways of doing things, inspire trends, and blaze trails that others follow. When you operate on this level, you open the door to greater financial rewards.

3. Are you passion-driven or profit-driven?

When you are passionate about what you do, you give 110 percent. Those who are most sought after for their skills are often those whose passion creates results that people need. Their passion for what they do sparks creativity, perseverance, and excellence—three traits that lead to long-term, consistent financial rewards. Success comes to those who are willing to stay the course despite challenges and distractions.

4. Do you know how to make money?

If the goal is to increase your income, then seek knowledge about how best to do that. Many people fail to earn more because they haven't made financial education a priority. While passion is a key to attracting financial rewards, making more money also means learning to live below your means, asking for what you are worth, investing, and spending wisely. Take classes, read financial books, and learn lessons from those who are where you want to be.

5. Are you willing to take a leap of faith?

Fear is the biggest obstacle to pursuing your dreams. Many people insist it is a lack of money, time, or resources, but it is often a fear of failure, rejection, or even a fear of success that holds a person back. What is it that you've been wanting to pursue that you've been hesitating about? Take baby steps if you have to, but be willing to step out in faith. If you do what you love patiently yet persistently, the rewards *will* come.

My Challenge to You

If you're launching a business, make a viable plan to take the entrepreneurial leap.

Coach Yourself

Ask yourself the five questions above and answer them honestly and thoroughly.

What have you learned from your money mistakes?

Learn from yesterday, live for today, hope for tomorrow.
ALBERT EINSTEIN

Point to ponder:

Researchers have discovered there are only three ways money can measurably boost your happiness: if you live below your means and have enough to pay your bills, if you make more than the people around you and don't feel pressured to keep up with the Joneses, and if you use it to make someone else happy. It is indeed better to give than to receive.

Whether it is too much debt, damaged credit, lack of savings, or not having enough income, financial challenges can be very stressful and discouraging. It is critical to your success strategy to focus on building a firm financial foundation to support your goals. In fact, it is a strong foundation in every area of your life that empowers you to build the life you truly want more easily.

Ask yourself "What are the three worst financial choices I have made in the past?" and "How could I avoid making similar choices in the future?" It is easy to beat yourself up for mistakes, but a better approach is to simply acknowledge poor choices and seek to make healthier choices starting today. Here are nine smart choices that will help you create a stronger financial foundation, less financial stress, and the freedom to enjoy your life more fully:

1. **Identify past choices that have led to financial frustration or stress and stop making those choices, starting today.**

   One of the most important choices you can make with your money is to learn from your past choices. Use failure and frustration as learning tools for future success.

2. **Pay off credit cards before other debt.**

   High balances on revolving debt, such as credit card debt, negatively impact your credit score more than loans that are scheduled to be paid off in a set number of months or years—such as a car loan, student loan, or mortgage. One of the fastest ways to improve your credit is to pay down or pay off your credit cards.

3. **Stop using your credit cards unless you can trust yourself to pay them in full each month.**

   The average American household carries more than $8,000 in credit card debt with no hope of paying it off in the next 60 days, according to the most recent statistics. Make a decision to live within your means, using the money you have rather than money you have to borrow.

4. **Change your lifestyle if necessary.**

   Sometimes building a strong financial foundation requires sacrifice. If you need to downsize your lifestyle so that you can become more financially strong, do it! It is empowering to make tough choices such as keeping your old car for a while longer, waiting to buy a bigger house, or curbing the shopping sprees while you save to buy your own home.

5. **Get insurance (health, life, home or renters', auto, and disability) that you feel confident will meet your needs in the event you need to use it.**

   No one ever expects a crisis, but it is comforting to know that in the event of one, your finances won't be completely destroyed.

An illness, fire, or accident is stressful enough. Make sure you are covered in the event of unfortunate circumstances.

6. Establish a financial cushion for 12 months of expenses.

Make this a priority goal and begin saving toward it, even if it takes you five years or more to reach your goal. Knowing that financial ruin is not a couple of paychecks away is a very empowering feeling. It will often keep you from making decisions out of fear and empower you to make decisions based on your purpose and vision.

7. Invest time in your own financial education.

One of the main causes of financial problems is what I call "financial illiteracy." Some companies make a great deal of money off of the financial ignorance of otherwise intelligent people. Spend two hours or more per month learning about wealth building, debt elimination, investing, and real estate. Read books or articles. Attend a seminar. Learn from those who handle their money well. The more financially literate you become, the better off you will be.

8. Have a vision. Set goals!

Create a vision for your finances. One of the reasons it is important to have a vision is because it serves as a reference point for where you are headed. When you are building toward something specific, it is easier to tell when you get off track. If you have no vision or goals, you often don't even realize you are on the wrong path until something goes terribly wrong!

9. Put money into proper perspective.

Having money can certainly make life easier, more convenient, and less stressful. But always remember this: If your biggest problems are money-related, consider yourself *very* blessed. Money problems can be fixed. There are other more important things in your life—your relationship with God and the people you care about, your health, and your integrity, just to name a few. Don't allow financial frustrations to ruin your relationships, cause you to be angry with God, do things that compromise your integrity, or stress you out to the point of causing high blood pressure, panic attacks, or other health problems. Count your blessings and remember that life's richest rewards will never be found in material things.

My Challenge to You

Decide what changes you need to make to build a stronger financial foundation for your life. Write them down and take action!

Coach Yourself

What past choices have led to financial stress or frustration in your life? What could you do differently to eliminate this stress and frustration in the future?

_____

_____

_____

_____

_____

_____

_____

Are you an emotional spender?

The number-one problem in today's generation and economy is the lack of financial literacy.

Alan Greenspan

Point to Ponder:

While incomes in the United States have doubled over the last few decades, happiness levels have not increased at all.

Even when times may be tough financially, some of us still don't have a handle on our spending. It's not for lack of knowledge. Often, it's a struggle with self-control. You went to the mall to buy a birthday gift for your niece, and walked out with a new pair of shoes for yourself. You've tried a budget, but somehow you always seem to find something to spend money on that wasn't in it. Can you relate? If so, consider these practical strategies to get your emotional spending under control:

1. Sleep on it.

If you think you just have to have it, whatever it is, make it your rule to sleep on your decision. Very few things are so urgent that you can't wait 24 hours to make your purchase.

2. Phone a friend.

You are far more likely to accomplish a goal if you tell someone else you've set it. So tell a friend about your goal to stop digging yourself into more credit card debt. Then when you find yourself about to make another purchase you can't afford, call them up and let them talk you down.

3. Never go shopping alone.

If you can't trust yourself to phone a friend, then don't go shopping alone. Have someone with you who will hold you accountable and remind you of your goals. Refuse to use "retail therapy" to deal with loneliness, boredom, or disappointments. Indulge in new hobbies that are active and foster connection and stronger relationships. Focus less on accumulating stuff and more on enjoying experiences with people and things that matter to you.

4. Plan for it.

Right now, take out a notepad and jot down the most important thing you need, and then the most important thing you want. How much will each cost? Jot that down. How long would it take you to save for each? Practice delayed gratification. It forces you to appreciate the true value of your money, which will help you spend your money more consciously.

5. Keep a picture of your goal in front of you.

To keep yourself reminded of your goal, put a photo that illustrates the goal in front of you. Whether on your refrigerator, in your purse, or on your bathroom mirror, make the vision plain and visible.

6. Take the credit cards out of your wallet.

As the saying goes, if you want to get out of the hole you're in, first, stop digging! If you're in debt, it's time to stop adding to your debt. And if you're an emotional spender, keep your impulse purchases to a minimum by leaving your credit cards at home. No need to make it easy to charge it.

7. Use cash.

There's something about forking over cash that makes you spend less. As simplistic as it sounds, one of the best ways to curb spending is to determine your budget for various expenses (i.e., lunch, groceries, clothing, etc.), then take out your budgeted amount in cash. While it can be easy to lose track of how much you spend when you swipe a credit or even a debit card, cash forces you to count and keep track of what you spend in a concrete way.

My Challenge to You

Make a decision to stop spending emotionally and start managing your money wisely.

Coach Yourself

At what times or in what situations are you most likely to spend emotionally? What are some ways in which you could reduce your temptation?

What would financial freedom look like for you?

If you can see the invisible, you can do the impossible.
BISHOP T.D. JAKES

Point to Ponder:

You need a vision for your finances just as you need a vision for your life. Get clear. Write it down. Then start walking toward it.

In a culture that often equates wealth with materialism, it's no wonder debt is out of control and savings are low. Answer these questions for yourself: Do you know how much you'll need for retirement? Are you on track to get there? If you lost your job or business dried up, how long could you pay your monthly expenses without borrowing? How about debt? If you have it, by what date will you eliminate it? Have you even imagined the prospect of having no debt?

You can build personal wealth and a greater sense of financial well-being, but it begins with imagination. Take a moment right now and close your eyes. Imagine what it would *feel* like to be financially free—no debt, house paid for, plenty saved, good income, and no financial worries. A good feeling, indeed, isn't it? For most Americans, the idea of financial freedom feels elusive—like a far-off dream too distant to attempt. But I challenge you to dream a bigger dream, and take steps to bring that dream to life.

Whether the dream of financial freedom is three years away or thirty, wouldn't it be worth it to start doing the things today that will leave you and those you love wealthier tomorrow? Here are five ways to do just that:

1. Envision yourself financially free.

It begins with imagining the possibility. With God, all things are possible. Begin seeing yourself in a better position financially. Rather than beating yourself up for mistakes or missteps, learn from them. Write down your money goals and post them where you will see them often. You need a financial vision.

2. Stop letting your emotions rule your money.

Do you spend to feel better? Out of guilt? To keep up with the Joneses? Emotional spending will curse your finances as you dig a deeper and deeper hole of debt.

3. Invest in more than a job.

Invest in education and knowledge that maximize your earning potential. But also invest in opportunities to create passive income by considering a business or solid real estate investment that can help you build recurring income over time.

4. Choose experiences over things.

Money spent on experiences with people brings more happiness than money spent on things. Consider that the next time you think you just have to have the latest gadget or new car. Building emotional wealth reaps meaningful rewards. Don't get trapped on the hedonic treadmill of wanting more and more stuff. Over time, you'll find it takes more and more to satisfy your appetite—and that includes more money.

5. Save consistently and unrelentingly.

If you were taught to save as a kid, you are ahead of the game! For many people, saving is a skill they must hone. While the amount you save is important, even more important is the consistency with which you save. Set up automatic deductions from your paycheck or checking account so you don't have to think about it. Learn to live on a smaller percentage of your income—just pretend you make less—and save the difference. Over time, you will see your wealth grow.

My Challenge to You

Make financial freedom your ultimate goal.

Coach Yourself

Reread the five strategies for building personal wealth. Which one resonates most as a step you need to take? What specifically will you do and when? What will financial freedom give you that you don't have right now? Why is that so important to you?

Are you financially on track to retire?

Before you speak, listen. Before you write, think.
Before you spend, earn. Before you invest, investigate.
Before you criticize, wait. Before you pray, forgive.
Before you quit, try. Before you retire, save.
Before you die, give.

WILLIAM A. WARD

Point to Ponder:

You can help your future self by taking steps in the present to make life easier years from now.

With the downward trend in pension plans over the last 30 years and decreasing confidence among Generation Xers (and younger) that Social Security will be around when they hit retirement age, many people need to wake up and take action when it comes to saving for retirement. And if you're the parent of anyone under the age of 40, you'll want to pass this message along. The majority of workers—56 percent—have less than $25,000 in retirement savings and 70 percent say they are behind in planning for retirement. Taking advantage of career options that maximize your security in retirement is more important than ever.

1. Get a reality check.

Retirement for our generation simply may not look like retirement for previous generations. Plan as though you will be entirely responsible because we don't know what changes will come in programs such as Social Security. Additionally, the number of people who are independent contractors has increased significantly—these are workers who don't even have an employer-sponsored 401(k), let alone a pension plan. Consider inflation too. The dollar will be worth less, taxes may increase, and a pension is far less likely. Ours will be the first generation in decades that may be primarily responsible for its own retirement. We don't learn how to succeed at this in schools. Employers are not required to teach it. You have to take charge. That means planning and taking action now.

2. Do the math!

Many people never actually sit down to do the math. In a recent poll, 42 percent of workers said they determined their retirement savings needs by guessing. When you are considering a job offer, always calculate the significance of retirement benefits. Negotiate with the goal of securing your financial future, not just making more money. If you continue on the path you are on, do you know how much you'll have and whether it will be enough for you to retire? Take a class, talk to an advisor, and invest in your financial education.

3. Have a dream. Set a goal date.

This is a critical step, and many people under 40 do not have a clear vision for what retirement looks like. Just like Baby Boomers were forever young, Generations X and Y can feel like retirement is so far off that it is hard to even imagine when they might like for it to come. With the end in mind, you can begin to develop your unique and personal strategy. This may entail service within organizations that will boost your retirement options. It may involve a plan to increase your income in the next few years so you can sock away more money. Your dream will make your action steps more clear. Be strategic and be open. Your plan may be entirely savings, but it may also include a business or real estate option that will get you to your retirement goal more effectively.

4. Aim to be debt-free.

We have become a country in which millions of people believe personal debt is normal and necessary. It's not. Becoming debt-free is possible, but the younger you are when you start, the easier it is to accomplish. Being debt-free gives you a sense of freedom and dramatically decreases the amount you'll need in order to be able to comfortably retire. In addition, it will give you more choices throughout your career if your choices are not entirely dependent upon your financial needs. Again, do the math. What would it take for you to become debt-free? When is your target date? This goal puts your salary negotiations and career transition options in a whole new light.

5. Maximize your company match.

This is free money. But oftentimes young people don't even understand what that means and how significantly it can impact their future. If you're reading this and you have young adults in your life, talk to them about retirement planning. Make sure they understand the basics. And if you're in that generation, consider this a wake-up call. There will come a day when you will want to retire—or may be forced to retire. Will you be ready? And will you be glad or regret the career choices you're making now?

My Challenge to You

Take charge of your financial future by saving enough for retirement.

Coach Yourself

How much will you need to comfortably retire and when do you plan to retire? What will you need to do now to ensure that money is available when you reach retirement age?

Coaching Toolkit

When you ask the right questions, you get the right answers. Use these questions to coach yourself in the area of business, career and finances. You may want to journal about them or work with a friend or coach to explore your answers.

- What is your most meaningful career goal right now?

- What are your greatest strengths?

- What would financial freedom look like for you?

- What lessons have you learned from your money mistakes?

- How would you describe your personal brand?

- What is your biggest challenge at work right now?

- What are three potential solutions to your biggest work challenge?

- Would your work best be described as a job, a career, or a calling?

- Looking back on your career, what would you have done differently had you known what you know now?

- Which emotion causes you to spend more?

- What do you want to be different in your career one year from now?

- What is your vision for where you will be professionally ten years from now?

- What do you need to begin doing now to prepare for that vision to become reality?

- In what way is the company you work for better off because you work there?

- Who are your career mentors or role models?

- Who has already achieved the vision you have for your career?

- What are the top three lessons you can glean from the person you just identified?

- What work-life boundaries do you need to put in place to maintain a sense of balance?

- What is your goal in terms of how much you want to earn annually in the coming year? How about three years from now?

- How much do you need in order to have an adequate emergency savings cushion (six to eight months' expenses)?

- What impact do you want to make on the people you work with and serve?

- What is the most stressful aspect of your work and what are at least three options for alleviating that stress?

- What do you want to do in retirement? Is there a second career you would pursue if you could? Will you continue in your current line of work but in a lesser capacity? Will you stop working altogether?

- What do you love most about your work?

- Are you doing work you love? If not, what do you love? Will you pursue it?

Part 3
Relationships

As iron sharpens iron, so one person sharpens ar
PROVERBS 27:17

Did You Know?

A groundbreaking 30-year Harvard study of more than 12,000 people showed that your odds of being happy increase 15 percent if someone in your social circle is happy. And if a friend of someone in your social circle is happy, you still boost your chances of being happy by 10 percent.

Think back to a time or a moment in your life when you were especially happy. It's a good bet that that moment involved at least one other person. Happiness doesn't occur in a vacuum. It happens in the context of relationships. A rich, happy life begins with rich, happy relationships.

Resilient people reach out. They have a supportive social network. They enjoy being part of a group. The happiest people have strong relationships and feel a sense of belonging. They interact frequently with others. They know their purpose is about the unique way in which they serve others and make a positive impact in the world—and they live it out daily in their connections with people.

How are you doing when it comes to your relationships? Check each statement that is true for you *today*.

☐ The relationships in my life are healthy and peaceful.

☐ I have at least three trustworthy people in my life in whom I can confide.

☐ I feel a sense of belonging, whether in the context of a family, work environment, or greater community.

☐ I have a personal friend or loved one to whom I am accountable. If I stray from my values, they have my permission to ask questions.

☐ I practice a random act of kindness at least once a week.

☐ I actively serve others—whether as a volunteer or by helping someone in my life who is in need.

☐ I listen to others without interrupting.

☐ I am not withholding forgiveness from anyone.

☐ There is no one in my life to whom I need to apologize.

☐ I feel heard. People care about what's going on with me.

☐ There are no relationships in my life that I feel the need to hide.

☐ People enjoy being around me.

☐ I am a great friend. I never tell others' secrets and am always supportive and respectful.

☐ I tell my loved ones I love them.

☐ I ask for help when I need it.

☐ I do not suffer from the comparison trap, measuring my worth by comparing myself to others.

☐ I am comfortable receiving love.

☐ I am easy to talk to.

☐ I do not require others to be perfect in order to be accepted by me.

☐ I like and love *me*. I have a healthy relationship with myself.

___ Total

Which statements weren't checked off? Turn these statements into goals for improving your relationships in the coming weeks and months!

Are you an effective communicator?

My dear brothers and sisters, take note of this:
Everyone should be quick to listen, slow to speak
and slow to become angry.

JAMES 1:19

Point to Ponder:

It is powerful, but all too rare, to truly feel heard.
Practice the art of listening so you can connect
quickly and deeply in your relationships.

Have you ever noticed that there are some people in your life with whom it is easier to communicate than others? Or have you been criticized at times for not listening, talking too much, or being overly sensitive? Sometimes it's hard to admit it when we need to improve, but there is always room to get better. And when it comes to communication, the better you are at it, the happier and smoother your relationships—and your life—will become.

The truth is, if you want to build a trusting and thriving relationship with someone—whether your spouse or coworker, your child or a neighbor—it is absolutely essential that your communication with them reflect four approaches:

1. Be quick to listen.

Ever notice how easy it is to get distracted when someone is talking? You begin to think about something similar that happened to you that you want to share, or you contemplate what you want to say next. Resist the urge. Practice listening without interrupting.

2. Be slow to speak.

Think of a time in the last week when you said something too quickly. Perhaps you wished you had worded it differently, or maybe that you had not said it at all. Emotions are often the culprit, whether you are energized and make a promise you can't keep or you're angry and speak words you later regret. Bite your tongue and give yourself time to compose your thoughts.

3. Be slow to be offended.

Just look at the news any day of the week. In recent years, it has been filled with apologies and misstatements, explanations and cover-ups. Sometimes others say things that are offensive with the intention of being offensive, and at other times a person simply needs the grace to be human. Don't look for reasons to be offended. Set boundaries, of course, but also be willing to give others the benefit of the doubt.

4. Be slow to anger.

This one can feel tough at times, especially when someone pushes your buttons. Anger is a normal emotion. The key to relationship success is in how you choose to handle it, and often this means taking a step back before expressing it. In my book *What's Really Holding You Back?* I talk about allowing your emotions to "school you, not rule you." Rather than allowing anger to automatically translate to harsh words or behavior, learn from it. It usually indicates a boundary has been crossed. What was the boundary? What could you do in the future to avoid a similar situation?

My Challenge to You

Be intentional about improving your personal communication skills.

Coach Yourself

In a relationship that is sometimes challenging to you, think back to your last interaction that did not go as you would have liked. In what ways were you quick to speak, slow to listen, easily offended, or too quickly angered? What could you change next time in order to communicate more effectively with that person?

What is your most difficult relationship?

Some of the biggest challenges in relationships come from the fact that most people enter a relationship in order to get something: they're trying to find someone who's going to make them feel good. In reality, the only way a relationship will last is if you see your relationship as a place that you go to give, and not a place that you go to take.

ANTHONY ROBBINS

Point to Ponder:

Every relationship offers you a life lesson that will empower you to grow. Especially in difficult relationships, be sure to get the lesson so you won't have to repeat it.

Have you ever encountered someone that you simply could not get along with, but you needed to deal with them on a regular basis anyway? When you have a choice in the matter, it is best to simply avoid being around difficult people. Of course, that isn't always a practical option—particularly if the difficult person is someone you work with, a neighbor, or even a relative. Dealing with difficult people does not always have to be difficult. It's all in how you *choose* to deal with them. Here are some ideas for dealing with the difficult people you encounter.

1. Be the bigger person.

You can't control how people behave, but you can control your response to their behavior. Understand that difficult people are usually unhappy people. They project their unhappiness onto others by their attitudes and actions. Difficult people have learned to get attention through their negativity and they thrive on getting a response out of you. If you do not allow them the satisfaction, you can often defeat them at their own game. They will soon stop being difficult with you and move on to the next person.

2. Return nasty behavior with calm behavior.

This will diffuse a situation rather than allowing it to escalate. Step away to give yourself time to calm down before responding. Whether it is simply a few seconds and a deep breath, a full 24 hours, or even longer, taking time to gather your thoughts allows you to regain control of your emotions. In other words, think before you speak. If you don't, you may end up saying or doing something that you will later regret.

3. Peaceably confront the issue.

Ask what can be done to mutually resolve the conflict. Maintain a positive attitude—even though this can be difficult. Remember, you are being the bigger person. Many difficult people are bullies, and do not expect people to confront their behavior—particularly not in a peaceful manner.

4. Treat people with respect, and demand respect for yourself.

Whether from a boss, coworker, family member, or friend, no one should have to tolerate disrespect or humiliation. People will treat you the way that you allow them to treat you. Set boundaries of respect and do not tolerate those boundaries being crossed. Expect to be treated with respect, and if you are not, bring up the issue with the offending person in a private discussion. You are only asking to be treated with the same respect that you give. When you allow others to disrespect you, you lose your self-respect. No relationship or job is worth that. If it is time to move on, be willing to do so. At some point, you must be willing to stand up for yourself.

5. Choose your battles wisely.

Your time and energy are valuable. Do not waste them by making an issue of every little thing that annoys you. Everything is not worth a confrontation. Learn to let some things go.

My Challenge to You

Don't allow a negative situation with a difficult person to escalate.

Coach Yourself

What's your most challenging relationship? Which of these strategies applies to you?

_____

_____

_____

_____

_____

_____

_____

_____

_____

Are you sure you're ready to say "I do"?

If any of you lacks wisdom, you should ask God,
who gives generously to all without finding fault,
and it will be given to you.

JAMES 1:5

Point to Ponder:

Intuition is intelligence. Never ignore it,
especially in life's most critical decisions.

Thinking about getting engaged? Daydreaming about saying "I do"? There are lots of questions to ask before you make a lifelong commitment, but here are three critical ones. Before you say "I do" to a potential spouse, make sure you can say "I do" to these...

1. If this person never changed, could you be content with him or her for the rest of your life?

You don't marry the person your mate could potentially become. You marry the person he or she *is*. Be brutally honest about his or her flaws and faults (keeping in mind that you have them too!). Then be honest with yourself. Could you live with those flaws and faults if they never changed? Most people don't change much, so don't count on it for your happiness.

2. Do you have a shared vision with your mate of your life together?

If you're going to spend the rest of your journey through life with someone, you'd better make sure you both want to journey to the same place. Do you share faith, friendship, and your dreams for the future? Without a shared vision, you will eventually bump up against some serious issues. In order to make it work, one of you may have to give up who you are in order to keep the relationship. The better solution would be to find the right mate in the first place—one with whom you can share in a vision that brings joy, peace, and purpose to you as a couple.

3. Do you love their character more than their career (or looks or money)?

Our culture tends to put more emphasis on *what* a person does for a living than *who* they are in character. Don't get caught up in the trap. Pay attention to your mate's everyday habits—does she lie? Does he do what he says he will when he says he will? Is she responsible? How does he treat his family? Is she respectful toward you, even when you disagree? Does he have your back?

If you can say "I do" to these three questions, you're on the right track. If not, slow down so you can make a wise decision about what you really want in a spouse. Ask yourself the hard questions now and you could save yourself heartache later.

My Challenge to You

When it comes to marriage, refuse to enter hastily. If there is *any* doubt, slow down.

Coach Yourself

If your partner never changed, could you be content with him or her for the rest of your life? Do you have a shared vision of your life together? Are you more in love with *who* they are on the inside or *what* they are on the outside?

Are you building authentic friendships?

Piglet sidled up to Pooh from behind.
"Pooh," he whispered.
"Yes, Piglet?"
"Nothing," said Piglet, taking Pooh's paw.
"I just wanted to be sure of you."

A.A. MILNE

Point to Ponder:

Friendships are vital to your well-being. Statistics show that who you choose to be close to determines a lot about who you become. Choose wisely.

Developing strong friendships is an important part of our personal and spiritual journey. And psychological research also shows that relationships and a sense of community are absolutely essential to your well-being. In fact, those who are happiest are those who report having a support structure of relationships that are fulfilling and healthy.

Consider this powerful Scripture about friendship:

Two are better than one, because they have a good return for their labor: If either of them falls down, one can help the other up. But pity anyone who falls and has no one to help them up. Also, if two lie down together, they will keep warm. But how can one keep warm alone? Though one may be overpowered, two can defend themselves. A cord of three strands is not quickly broken (Ecclesiastes 4:9-12).

Friends strengthen one another. God designed us for companionship rather than isolation. Our core purpose in life cannot be fulfilled except in the context of relationships because we are each called to serve others in some way. You need true friends. And like any authentic relationship, a friendship must be built and maintained.

While you don't choose your family, you can choose your friends. So it is important to choose wisely. Consider strong friendships a part of your definition of success. Here are four ways God coaches us about friendships. Consider the state of your friendships and create your own personal action steps based on these Scriptures:

1. Go for quality, not quantity.

"One who has unreliable friends soon comes to ruin, but there is a friend who sticks closer than a brother" (Proverbs 18:24). The New Living Translation renders the same verse this way: "There are 'friends' who destroy each other, but a real friend sticks closer than a brother." It is not the quantity of your friendships that matters, but the quality. You don't need a lot of friends who are really just acquaintances with whom you share no true companionship. Instead focus on developing meaningful friendships with other people who share your values, show concern and respect for you, and with whom you enjoy spending time. When you desire new friendships or seek to strengthen the ones you have, remember that, as the New King James Version translates that same verse, "a man who has friends must himself be friendly." Extend your love and friendship to others, even if you feel vulnerable at first. This is how true friendships develop. Reach out and do something friendly for a person who is already a good friend or someone with whom you feel led to develop a stronger friendship.

2. Seek authenticity in your friendships.

"Wounds from a friend can be trusted, but an enemy multiplies kisses" (Proverbs 27:6). Authentic friendships are built on trust.

When someone is your true friend, they have your best interests at heart. This means they should be able to speak the truth in a spirit of love. It may hurt, but words that are difficult to hear can also help you grow. Enemies, even though they may shower you with lavish praise and kisses, are deceitful. They may be jealous or seeking to get close to you only to hurt you or get what they want. Pray for discernment about who your true friends are and cherish them, even when what they have to say is unpleasant to hear. Thumb through your mental Rolodex of friends and identify the friendships that are truly authentic. When you need solid advice or an important opinion, these are the friends to talk to. If there is a friendship that is not authentic, make a decision about whether to strengthen it or allow it to consume less of your time.

3. Seek at least one friendship with an elder who is older and wiser.

"Similarly, teach the older women to live in a way that honors God. They must not slander others or be heavy drinkers. Instead, they should teach others what is good. These older women must train the younger women…" (Titus 2:3-4 NLT). Seek not only peer relationships, but at least one mentor relationship with a person who is older and wiser. There is nothing like the advice of someone who has "been there and done that." Who do you look up to who could fulfill this role in your life? In what ways could you also be a blessing to him or her? Identify a mentor relationship that you want to build and maintain. If you do not know anyone who fits the bill, make it a goal to put yourself in an environment in which you can meet such a role model.

4. Choose your friends wisely.

"As iron sharpens iron, so one person sharpens another," says Proverbs 27:17. King Solomon also advises, "Do not make friends with a hot-tempered person, do not associate with one easily angered, or you may learn their ways and get yourself ensnared" (Proverbs 22:24-25). Choose your friends wisely. They can either make you better by challenging and encouraging you or make you weaker by influencing you negatively. Which friends in your life tempt you to live below your potential? Whether it's gossip, cheating, worldliness, complacency, or any other behavior that is destructive, being around people whose actions are not aligned with your values will make it much harder for you to achieve your personal potential. Seek friends who sharpen you. Be intentional about the friendships you choose to build and maintain. When it comes to your closest friendships, choose healthy friendships with people who want to please God.

My Challenge to You

Make a decision to create and maintain authentic friendships.

Coach Yourself

What actions will you commit to taking to build and maintain authentic friendships? When will you take those actions?

_____

_____

_____

_____

_____

_____

_____

How well do you take a compliment?

*When receiving a compliment, don't insult the
giver by declining it, but express your
gratitude with a "thank you."*

VALORIE BURTON

Point to Ponder:

*Compliments are a gift. If you begin seeing them
as such, you'll respond accordingly.*

Imagine for a moment that a thoughtful person decided to give you a beautifully wrapped gift, complete with a satin ribbon tied in a pretty bow. How would you respond? Would you ignore them and decline to even acknowledge the gift? Would you rebuff the giver and tell them they were being ridiculous to do something so kind? Or would you tell them they're giving the gift to the wrong person and suggest someone more deserving?

You'll probably agree that none of these three options is particularly gracious. In fact, they are downright rude. And yet, as a coach, I notice that this is exactly how many people handle the gift of a compliment. I challenge you to receive compliments graciously and express gratitude for them.

When someone offers you a compliment, respond as though they just handed you a beautifully wrapped gift. Whether you deserve it or agree with it or not, acknowledge the thoughtfulness of the gesture. When someone says, "Your hair looks great today," don't respond with, "I was in such a rush this morning—I barely had time to do it!" When a coworker acknowledges, "You did a fantastic job on that presentation," resist saying, "I should have practiced more. I forgot some of the points I wanted to make!" Even when everything in you wants to explain it away, take a breath and say two simple words, "Thank you." Don't add any more words to your statement. Not, "Thank you, but it was really nothing" or, "Thanks, but you did a much better job than I did." Simply say "Thank you."

When I receive a compliment I am grateful, not because I think I'm so great and deserving, but because a compliment reminds me of how blessed I am. It is an acknowledgment of a gift or talent I've been given, or an accomplishment I've had the opportunity to achieve. Love and kindness come in many forms—and a compliment is one of them. Think of a compliment as a little piece of God's love flowing through someone else. Don't deflect it. Receive it with open arms. Be encouraged by it. And remember these three things the next time someone compliments you:

1. You have attributes worthy of acknowledgment.

When you allow others to acknowledge good things about you, you are acknowledging that there are, in fact, good things about you! Be thankful for them, and thankful that others appreciate them.

2. Humility does not preclude you from accepting a compliment.

Humility acknowledges where your blessings come from, and is gracious and thankful for the thoughtfulness of others. Accepting a compliment doesn't mean you think there is no room for improvement. It's simply an opportunity to express your gratitude.

3. Refusal to accept a compliment is often a sign of a struggle to value oneself.

You may insist that the things you are complimented for are no big deal. Just because something comes easily to you doesn't mean it is not valuable. There are innate gifts you possess that are meaningful and valuable to others. Don't discount them because they come naturally. Simply be grateful.

My Challenge to You

Learn to accept a compliment!

Coach Yourself

In what areas of your life do you find it difficult to take a compliment? How could you begin acknowledging your gratitude in that area? How will you respond the next time you receive the gift of a compliment?

_____

_____

_____

_____

_____

_____

_____

_____

_____

Do you know how to give a great compliment?

I can live for two months on a good compliment.
MARK TWAIN

Point to Ponder:
*An authentic compliment is an opportunity
for heartfelt connection.*

We just talked about how to receive a compliment. But did you know that there is a way to give a compliment that can be truly meaningful for the receiver? It can revolutionize how people feel about you because when a compliment is given well, it touches the core of who that person is. It affirms the best aspects of who they are and what they are made of. A powerful compliment is a gift you give to others—a way of expressing gratitude and good will in the world.

Instead of simply, "Good job on that project," tell them how their contribution to the project made it better—something like, "Your hard work really shined through. It's obvious you've been at this a long time." Rather than, "That's a nice shirt," be specific about what it is about the shirt that makes it nice on that person. For example, "The color of that shirt really brings out your eyes."

A great compliment acknowledges the positives about another person. This acknowledgment is powerful because so often, good things go unmentioned or unnoticed. We can become experts at pointing out what's wrong with something or someone while taking for granted what's right.

Here are four simple guidelines for giving a powerful compliment:

1. Be specific.

Memorable compliments are specific. Don't be vague when you give a compliment. Notice what it is that compelled you to want to give the compliment in the first place, and then articulate it to the person.

2. Acknowledge their character.

When complimenting an accomplishment, don't just acknowledge what the person did. Acknowledge who they had to be in order to accomplish it. In other words, what did it take for them to make it happen? Point to a person's character traits, such as perseverance, kindness, thoughtfulness, loyalty, humor, calmness, creativity, or courage. For example, "It took a lot of courage for you to speak up like that" or, "You are so creative. I love the way you put together your outfit."

3. Be authentic.

If you don't really mean the compliment, don't give it. Everyone has some character strength or gift worthy of acknowledgment. Make a habit of finding the good in others. Sometimes you may be the only person to point it out. Your authentic compliment will be an extraordinary gift for that person because they rarely hear something positive about themselves from others.

4. Express your appreciation.

When complimenting someone about something they did that benefitted you, be direct in your praise. "It meant a lot to me that…" or, "I appreciate you for…" You might assume that the people in your life know you appreciate them, but don't leave them wondering. Say so.

My Challenge to You

Give a great compliment!

Coach Yourself

Think of someone in your life whom you have not complimented in a while. What specifically would you like to compliment them about? How could you word the compliment in a
way that will make it authentic and acknowledge the essence of
who they are?

_____

_____

_____

_____

_____

_____

_____

_____

_____

Are you easy to love?

Even the rich are hungry for love, for
being cared for, for being wanted, for having
someone to call their own.

MOTHER TERESA

Point to Ponder:

What's it like to be in a relationship with you? Putting your-
self in others' shoes can help you see how your
habits and behaviors impact others.

I bought a cute card for my goddaughter recently. Her birthday falls
on Valentine's Day and the card jokingly said, "People born on Valentine's Day are easier to love." It occurred to me that some people really
are easier to love, aren't they? Why is that? I think it is because some
people are better at loving others. Because they express love in healthy
ways on a consistent basis, they also attract love into their lives. It is a
simple principle most of us have been taught repeatedly: What you
sow, you will also reap.

I would like to serve as your loving reminder of what it means to
love someone. These are seven straightforward, at times difficult, but
always effective strategies for loving others—and experiencing more
love in your life. The apostle Paul wrote about them in his first letter
to the Corinthians, chapter 13. We often hear the Scripture recited
at weddings. Meditate on these seven principles. Find new ways to
express love on a daily basis and strengthen your daily interaction with
others—whether loved ones or strangers, coworkers or neighbors. The
greatest use of your life is to love. When you apply this kind of love to
a situation, it never fails.

1. Love is patient.

People won't always do what you want when you want them to. Practice being patient—whether with your children, your significant other, or the grocery store clerk who takes too long to ring up your order. Everything happens for a reason—and that includes the timing of when things happen. Be patient and learn the lesson that comes in the process of enduring the wait. Sometimes the lesson is simple: Slow down and enjoy life.

2. Love is kind.

Every single day, choose to be kind. Ask yourself each morning, "How could I be a blessing to someone today?" Whether it is a kind word, a loving gesture, or helping someone in need, seek ways to be kind daily. Not only will it be a blessing to those you encounter, but it will feel good deep in your soul.

3. Love does not envy.

There will always be someone who appears to have more or to be doing better. Make a decision not to be envious of others, but in every circumstance of life find a reason to be thankful. Jealousy poisons your attitude, builds resentment, and can ruin relationships. Rather than envying others, learn from them. Even be inspired by them. And simultaneously, choose to be content with what you have while you journey toward something better.

4. Love does not boast. Love is not proud.

Resist the temptation to boast about yourself, your accomplishments, or your loved ones. It often only makes others feel "less than," which, of course, is not an expression of love. Practice humility. Allow your accomplishments to speak for themselves. Others often notice your good work and deeds, even without you having to make a big deal of them. In fact, it is far more attractive to simply *be* great than to try to convince others of your greatness.

5. Love is not rude. Love is not easily angered.

We've all had our moments when our behavior has been less than considerate. Next time you feel the urge to be rude, inconsiderate, or to jump to conclusions, stop yourself. Take a deep breath and ask what a more loving response to the situation might look like. That doesn't mean that you allow others to walk all over you. You can speak the truth to people in a very matter-of-fact way without being rude. Be considerate of others' feelings and be willing to give people the benefit of the doubt.

6. Love keeps no record of wrongs.

Have you ever known someone who remembered every mistake you ever made or everything you ever did wrong? As you have grown and become a better person, all they can remember is the person you used to be. It is very frustrating and you may even find yourself ready to distance yourself from that person. Learn from the past behavior of others—and protect yourself accordingly, when necessary—but resist the temptation to continually bring up everything someone has done wrong. Love others by urging and encouraging them toward a better future, not defining them by their past.

7. Love rejoices in the truth.

So often, it seems, we are afraid of the truth. When something is wrong, we pretend everything is okay. Often both parties will pretend even when they each know there is a problem. One of the most important love skills you can learn is honesty. Refuse to live lies or to accept lies as truth. Have truthful conversations with yourself and others. It allows you to get to the core of issues faster. It empowers others to trust you. It relieves the stress of tiptoeing around the real issues. Learn to speak the truth in a spirit of love and kindness, and your life will be richer and more fulfilling.

My Challenge to You

In a situation that is challenging or frustrating to you, find a way to express love. Perhaps it's time to call a truce, forgive someone who has done you wrong, tell the truth, or be more patient. What could you do to be more loving?

Coach Yourself

What makes the person most important to you feel loved? What are three ways that you could incorporate more of it into your interaction with this person? What makes you feel loved? How could you communicate this in a loving way?

Do you know the key to boosting your kids' confidence?

There are only two lasting bequests we can give our children—one is roots, the other wings.
STEPHEN COVEY

Point to Ponder:
The work you do as a parent will echo for generations to come.

Does your child get great grades or do they lag behind their classmates, struggling to stay motivated in the face of another disappointing report card? As a parent, one of the best things you can do is boost your kids' confidence so they persevere through disappointing test scores or flat-out bad grades. Research shows that kids who fall into certain traps when explaining bad events, such as a failed test or poor grade, are more likely to give up and stop trying to do better. It's called explanatory style, a term coined by University of Pennsylvania psychologist Dr. Martin Seligman. You, as a parent, can help boost your children's confidence by paying attention to what they say after they've failed at something—and encouraging them to change their explanatory style. Doing so will boost their confidence and, ultimately, their performance.

There are three signs to look for in how your children explain why something didn't go well—whether a test, a game, or even a spat with a friend. Think back to the last time your child didn't do well at something. Did their explanation reflect any of these three pitfalls?

1. It's Personal: It's me. It's all my fault!

Kids (and even adults!) who blame themselves entirely for their failures without pinpointing some of the changeable circumstances that contributed to the failure are less motivated to try harder—and they are more likely to have low self-esteem. "I'm stupid, that's why I got a D on the test" is a personal explanation. "I didn't study much, the teacher didn't explain the material well, and I was hungry because I skipped breakfast" are external explanations. And they are all things you can do something about the next time around.

2. It's Permanent: I never do well on tests. I always screw up.

If your child uses "always" and "never" to explain a failure, boost their confidence by helping them remember a time when the opposite was true. "What about the English test you did well on last week? You didn't mess up on that." Help them see failures and mistakes as temporary situations that offer life lessons. When they use words such as "always" and "never," get them to change those words to "sometimes" and "lately."

3. It's Pervasive: I can't do anything right. Everything I do goes wrong.

Lastly, teach your kids to see failure as a specific event so that a loss of confidence at school doesn't spill over into other areas of life. Every kid has different strengths. As a culture, we tend to put a lot of emphasis on grades. In the real world, there are kids who drop out of college (ever heard of Bill Gates?) who are immensely talented, but just not in the ways measured by traditional academia. Discover your child's strengths and celebrate them. Help them do well at school, but also make a big deal out of what they do well (music, leadership, sports, making friends) outside the classroom.

My Challenge to You

Be intentional about boosting your child's confidence.

Coach Yourself

In what areas does your child lack confidence? The last time they experienced a setback or disappointment, which of these three pitfalls did they tend to fall into? Using your new knowledge of these three pitfalls, what conversation will you have with your child and when?

_____

_____

_____

_____

_____

_____

_____

_____

_____

_____

Do you pass this love test?

Happy marriages are based on a deep friendship.
By this I mean a mutual respect for and
enjoyment of each other's company.

JOHN GOTTMAN

Point to Ponder:

Negativity has a stronger impact than positivity.
In a marriage, it takes five positive interactions
to undo one negative.

How do you know if your marriage will stand the test of time? What if there were a formula that predicted whether or not you could make it through tough times? According to a group of researchers and psychologists at the Relationship Research Institute, there is a way to answer these questions with more than 90 percent accuracy. In studies of over 500 couples, analyzed for their negative and positive interactions with each other during discussions on thorny topics such as money and budgeting, the researchers predicted with 94 percent accuracy who would still be married a decade later. What's the secret?

Even when the conversation gets heated or difficult, the couples who stay married have at least five positive interactions for every negative. When couples fall below this five-to-one ratio, they tend to divorce within ten years. So what does this mean for your love life? Negative words and emotions are more powerful than positive, so one negative must be balanced with at least five positives.

If he overspent for the third month in a row despite your

agreed-upon budget, don't let the discussion spiral downward into attacks on his character and a laundry list of everything else he's done wrong this month. Stick to the issue at hand and the outcomes you want, such as predictability in your budget or the ability to trust him when he makes a commitment.

Achieving the five-to-one ratio isn't just about words, but about connection. If there is something he's done well, acknowledge it. If he struggles with balancing the checkbook, empathize and discuss a solution. A show of empathy amounts to a positive interaction and so does the acknowledgment of something good. Holding hands at some point during the discussion would be another positive, for example. When your spouse knows that you're upset about the behavior, but still value him in that moment as your partner, he will be more open to making an effort to improve.

Importantly, the five-to-one ratio isn't all about just being positive. The ratio has an upper limit, according to other research psychologists. When the positive-to-negative ratio exceeds eleven to one, the "formula" no longer works. No relationship can be all positive, all the time. Couples must be able to tell each other the truth when something is wrong, share frustrations, and be angry. Staying together isn't just about being happy all the time. It's about making sure the negatives don't overpower the positives.

My Challenge to You

Be aware of the effect of both negative and positive interactions with your spouse.

Coach Yourself

What is the positive-to-negative ratio in my relationship? What can I do to improve that ratio?

How good are you at making new friends?

Shared joy is a double joy; shared sorrow is half a sorrow.
SWEDISH PROVERB

Point to Ponder:
*Being able to step out of your comfort zone
and connect with new people
is a sign of resilience.*

Research shows that the number of people the average American calls a close friend or confidant has decreased by 50 percent since 1986. There are many reasons, but one may be mobility. For various reasons, we move around more and find ourselves starting over more than ever. In your twenties, a time when fewer people are settled down with families, it can be easier to find time for and make new friends. But after the age of 30, many find it increasingly difficult to meet new people and establish relationships. If that's you, use these five strategies to establish and build meaningful friendships:

1. Reach out to old friends.
If you've recently moved to a new city, do you know someone who lives there now? Do you have friends who used to live there and can make introductions? Use your existing connections to make new connections. And if you're in the same old city, don't hesitate to reach out to old friends you've lost touch with if your values and interests are aligned.

2. Get involved in an activity you love.

Notice I said "an activity you love." That's because meaningful friendships are often built—or at least started—on a common interest. Whether it's a shared alma mater, a sport you love, or a charity you volunteer with, you'll find like-minded people in places where you love to be. Likewise, if you spend time doing stuff you don't enjoy but think you should, you can sabotage your efforts by connecting with people who don't share your interests and passions.

3. Make the first move.

Meet someone interesting at an event? Ask them to lunch or invite them to do something. Did they mention an interest of theirs? Send an e-mail and share a tidbit that is relevant to them. Start communicating. Over time, a friendship can blossom.

4. Host something fun.

A dinner party. Girls' night out. A celebration of some sort. Find reasons to be social and bring people together. Invite others to bring along a friend or two—a great way to meet even more people.

5. Take a look around the office.

You spend a lot of time at work, and it can be a great place to make friends. In fact, Gallup research has shown that those who say they have a best friend at work are more productive and have higher morale. And if you work from home, get involved in your professional associations or networks that expose you to people in your field, especially if you love your line of work.

My Challenge to You

Choose one of the five strategies above to make a new friend in the next two weeks.

Coach Yourself

Think about it. How will making a new friend or two enhance your life?

_____

_____

_____

_____

_____

_____

_____

_____

_____

_____

_____

_____

_____

_____

Is it time for a get-together?

*I'm glad we had the times together just to laugh and sing
a song. Seems like we just got started and then before you
know it, the times we had together were gone.*

Dr. Seuss

Point to Ponder:

*In a survey of over 400 professional women,
55 percent said they had not had a friend
inside their home in over two months.*

When is the last time you had a friend over for a visit? When researching for my book *How Did I Get So Busy?* I was stunned when 55 percent of respondents to that question told me it had been more than two months since they had had someone over! Why? Life is too busy. There's so much to do that friendships get crowded out. If busyness has become your excuse for not getting together with friends and loved ones, it's time to reclaim your schedule and make time for some fun and friendship.

This week, I challenge you to make it a priority to get together with some friends it's time to reconnect with. Make it simple. Make it fun. Make it happen. Here are a few ideas:

1. Have a game night.

Dust off the board games from the top shelf of the closet, hook up your Wii, and let the games begin. Having a game night is a great way to get friends or family together for something more than staring at a movie or television—activities that don't encourage conversation or interaction. Rediscover your inner kid, and have fun.

2. Order pizza.

Invite a few friends over, order pizza, and just hang out. How about tonight? Or this coming weekend?

3. Celebrate something!

Milestones, birthdays, wins—find reasons to celebrate. It's a great excuse to get together. A neighbor recently had a get-together to celebrate returning home after a long trip. Another threw a party to celebrate a friend emerging successfully from a health challenge. Make a habit of finding reasons to get together and celebrate life. It's a contagious form of gratitude that brings people together.

4. Have an ice cream social.

Whether the occasion is a holiday gathering or a barbecue, my friends know I'll be making them made-to-order ice cream sundaes. The first time I made them for friends, it was just a time-saving alternative to baking a cake! The sundaes were a hit, and I've been doing it ever since. Host your own ice cream social on a weekend afternoon—no cooking required.

5. Just stop by.

With some friends and family, getting together couldn't be more simple. And yet so many people take for granted the friends and family that live nearby. Stop by for a visit this afternoon or this week, just to say hi.

My Challenge to You

Reconnect with friends this week. Have fun!

Coach Yourself

Who would you like to connect with, but haven't in a while?
When will you do it? What would you like to do to get together?

Is it time to stop complaining and solve the problem?

Do everything without grumbling or arguing.
PHILIPPIANS 2:14

Point to Ponder:

*When problems arise, resilient people determine
what is within their control to fix and go
about the business of fixing it.*

Perhaps the change that's nudging you isn't about a new career, a new relationship, or a new home. It may not be a major change that you need to make but a change in how you approach the everyday issues that frustrate you. Changing directions may be about changing your attitude to a proactive one.

What do you find yourself complaining about in your day-to-day life? A moody client, boss, or employee? Messy spouse? Clutter? Poor service? When it comes to learning and growing, a useful tool for making meaningful changes can be your own complaints. After all, the things that you complain about are the things that, if changed, have the potential to dramatically improve the quality of your life.

In a world sometimes filled with negativity and complaining, it can be tempting at times to complain for the sake of complaining. Instead, use your complaints about your life as an opportunity to improve your life. Ask, "What could be done about it? What request or change could I make to eliminate this complaint from my life?"

If your complaint is bad traffic, for example, you may simply have to make a decision to quit complaining about it. Make a decision to relax in traffic, accept it as part of your day, and find a constructive way to use your drive time—like listening to relaxing music or audiobooks or catching up with friends or family (on your hands-free phone, of course!).

I have found that complaining without taking action to do something about it is very disempowering—not to mention unproductive. When you stop *having* problems and start *solving* them, your life becomes more productive, joyful, and powerful.

I challenge you to notice the message that your complaints are sending you. Complaints often indicate that an expectation or need is not being met. Complaints continue to plague you when you do not make requests of others to change or do not challenge yourself to make changes that will turn the problem around.

1. Make a list of ten complaints.

I challenge you to make a list of ten complaints in your life (or more, if you have them!). Your complaints are things that just are not going as you would like to see them. From the friend who drains your energy with negativity to the client or boss with unrealistic or unfair expectations to the computer that is on its last leg, make a list of everything that drains your energy, unsettles or annoys you, or detracts from your quality of life.

2. Make a list of ten requests.

What requests could you make to address each complaint? Even if your complaint seems beyond your control to change, write it down anyway. If you have a complaint you feel at a loss to resolve, you can always take it directly to God in prayer. You may be surprised to see them resolved—sometimes even more quickly than the ones you feel you have more control over. Keep in mind that some of your requests will be of yourself. You may need to challenge yourself to do something differently in a particular area of your life or to take a specific action to resolve the problem.

3. Follow through with specific requests to solve the problem.

Asking for what you want is one of the keys to success. Often change is nothing more than a conversation away. (For step-by-step instructions on the best way to succeed at asking for what you want, read the chapter on this subject in *What's Really Holding You Back?*) Have you been clear about your expectations? Have you voiced your dissatisfaction and requested a specific change or solution? Until you do, you may find yourself stuck with the same complaints indefinitely. Tired of a neighbor or coworker, or someone crossing your boundaries? Speak up! Ask them to make a specific change. You can simply say, "What you are doing is causing a problem. Would you please not do that anymore?" You may have to practice your words before you say them if you are shy about speaking up for yourself, but whatever it takes, take action by verbalizing specific requests.

My Challenge to You

Stop complaining and become proactive about resolving the things that cause you problems. Write down your list of complaints, beginning with your biggest one. Then create a solution and move forward in implementing it!

Coach Yourself

What is the payoff I get when I complain rather than taking steps to fix the problem? What will it take for me to make a shift to being proactive?

Coaching Toolkit

When you ask the right questions, you get the right answers. Use these questions to coach yourself in the area of relationships. You may want to journal about them or work with a friend or coach to explore your answers.

- How are others' lives better because they cross your path?

- What is it like to be in a relationship with you?

- What makes your spouse feel loved?

- What makes your children feel loved?

- What makes you feel loved?

- In a current relationship challenge, what would happen if you dropped the need to be right?

- What relationship in your life most needs to be strengthened?

- What could you do to mend a relationship in your life that is currently broken?

- What would happen if you insisted on talking less and listening more?

- In a current challenge that you find yourself complaining about, what could you do to solve the problem?

- Who are your three closest friends and confidants—people you trust and enjoy?

- What is your ideal vision for how often you'd like to get together with friends?

- Who in your life needs more of your attention right now?

- At work, what relationships do you want to further develop and what could you do to facilitate that?

- In what way do you make a positive impact on the community around you?

- With whom would you most like to build a relationship in the coming year? What is the purpose in building this relationship?

- Which relationships are draining your energy? What are you willing to do about it and when?

- What payoff are you receiving for remaining in a friendship that is unhealthy?

- If you are married, what are the top five signs that your marriage is thriving and healthy?

- If you are single, what are your non-negotiable standards for considering a romantic relationship with someone?

- Which couple serves as your relationship role model and what lessons have you learned from their example?

- What past challenges negatively impact your interactions in present relationships? What are you doing to overcome those challenges so you can be free from your past?

- What are you *afraid* will happen if you open yourself to a new relationship?

- What do you *hope* will happen if you open yourself to a new relationship?

- Who in your life loves you for being you? Who in your life is more interested in what you do, who you know, or your accomplishments?

Part 4
Hope and Inspiration

*Now faith is confidence in what we hope for and
assurance about what we do not see.*

HEBREWS 11:1

Did You Know?

People with higher self-efficacy (a belief that you can
do it) set more difficult goals for themselves and are
more likely to *be* committed and *stay* committed, sus-
tain their efforts even in the face of negative feedback,
and make course corrections.

In the face of temptation so many of us can be tempted to lose hope. But when you stop hoping, a part of you dies. Think of each hope or dream you have for your life as a lit candle that illuminates your soul and lights your pathway. Hope compels you to move forward. It motivates you to take action. But each time you allow yourself to despair, one of those candles is extinguished. Over time, the flames of inspiration will burn out if you are not intentional about rekindling your hope.

Fortunately, hope is a choice. And you can begin today to hope again. In this section, we'll talk about doing just that—hoping and finding inspiration in the experiences of life.

When hope is rekindled, optimism must soon follow. Even if you are not naturally optimistic, research is clear that optimism can be learned. So keep an open mind and let yourself take hold of the authentic hopes that are calling for your attention.

Just how optimistic and hopeful are you? Check each statement below that is true for you *today*.

- [ ] I do not get discouraged easily.

- [ ] Despite the disappointments I have suffered, I have hope that my future will be satisfying.

- [ ] I am inspired by others' stories of success because they give me hope that I can do it too.

- [ ] There is nothing in my life that I am settling for.

- [ ] When I succeed, I do not downplay or dismiss the effort I put forth, saying things like "Oh, it was just a lucky break."

- [ ] I believe in myself.

- [ ] I have a clear set of goals for my professional and personal life.

- [ ] I have a clear vision of what I want my relationships to look like.

- [ ] I have a clear set of financial goals and a plan to get there.

- [ ] I have inspiring health and fitness goals that compel me to push forward.

- [ ] I pray regularly.

- [ ] I sense an inner voice, the voice of the Holy Spirit, that often guides me in my life.

☐ Even when things get tough, I do not give up hope.

☐ I see challenges as temporary and expect to work through them.

☐ I feel confident most of the time.

☐ I get excited about my vision for my life and the future that's ahead.

☐ If I wanted to make an unconventional change in my life, such as changing careers or deciding to become a parent later in life, I would give myself permission to go for it!

☐ As a leader at home, work, or in the community, I am good at helping people see the vision for where we are headed.

☐ I listen to my intuition and follow it, even when I feel fear.

☐ I look for the good in every situation.

___ Total

What would Jesus ask?

Ask and it will be given to you; seek and you will find;
knock and the door will be opened to you.

Matthew 7:7

Point to Ponder:

When you meditate on divine wisdom, you can
go deeper by asking yourself empowering
questions based on that wisdom.

It is both biblical and practical to seek coaching and mentoring from other people. Proverbs 15:22 says, "Plans fail for lack of counsel, but with many advisers they succeed." The advisers we choose—coaches, mentors, counselors—should offer counsel that reflects the wisdom of the Word of God. But you often don't need others for counsel you seek. You need the ultimate life coach, *God Himself.*

I like to use my Bible as a personal coaching tool. Jesus coached through both words and actions. He also gave lessons on success, leadership, money, marriage, anxiety, relationships, emotions, and more.

It is amazing that no matter what you are going through, no matter the frustration or triumph, there is biblical guidance that applies directly to the situation. Consider for a moment a challenge you'd like an answer to. Write it here:

In this challenge and others you face in the future, consider these ten coaching questions derived directly from Jesus's teachings in the book of Matthew to help you uncover the answer you've been searching for:

1. **Coaching Question:** What could you do to maximize this moment so that you have no regrets tomorrow?
Jesus: "Therefore do not worry about tomorrow, for tomorrow will worry about itself" (Matthew 6:34).

2. **Coaching Question:** What temptation do you need to actively pray for help to overcome?
Jesus: "Watch and pray so that you will not fall into temptation. The spirit is willing, but the flesh is weak" (Matthew 26:41).

3. **Coaching Question:** In what way is it time to stop selling yourself short?
Jesus: "Do not give dogs what is sacred; do not throw your pearls to pigs. If you do, they may trample them under their feet, and turn and tear you to pieces" (Matthew 7:6).

4. **Coaching Question:** What is the personal struggle that has most sabotaged your success?
Jesus: "Why do you look at the speck of sawdust in your brother's eye and pay no attention to the plank in your own eye?... First take the plank out of your own eye, and then you will see clearly to remove the speck from your brother's eye" (Matthew 7:3,5).

5. **Coaching Question:** What are you afraid of?
Jesus: "You of little of faith, why are you so afraid?" (Matthew 8:26).

6. **Coaching Question:** In what way could you trust God more in the challenge or opportunity you face right now?
Jesus: "Do you believe that I am able to do this?" (Matthew 9:28).

7. **Coaching Question:** What burden do you need to surrender to God today?
Jesus: "Come to me, all you who are weary and burdened, and I will give you rest" (Matthew 11:28).

8. Coaching Question: What small seed do you need to plant right now so it can take root and grow into a powerful vision for the future?

Jesus: "The kingdom of heaven is like a mustard seed, which a man took and planted in his field. Though it is the smallest of all seeds, yet when it grows, it is the largest of garden plants and becomes a tree, so that the birds come and perch in its branches" (Matthew 13:31-32).

9. Coaching Question: Which role model overcame the challenge you now face and offers an example you can follow?

Jesus: "If the blind lead the blind, both will fall into a pit" (Matthew 15:14).

10. Coaching Question: Instead of looking for what you can get out of a situation, ask, "What is it that God wants me to give?"

Jesus: "The greatest among you will be your servant. For those who exalt themselves will be humbled, and those who humble themselves will be exalted" (Matthew 23:11-12).

Of course, you can begin to create your own coaching questions by reading His words and pondering the relevant questions they pose for your life. Ask open-ended questions that provoke thought and challenge you to answer more than a simple *yes* or *no*. Make a game of it. Pray for help to discover the right questions to ask yourself. Then honestly answer them on your personal journey of spiritual growth and well-being.

My Challenge to You

Rather than only seeking others' opinions about how you should handle a personal obstacle or situation, see what the Bible has to say about it.

Coach Yourself

Think of a challenge you're facing right now. What wisdom does God offer on the subject? What personal question arises from that wisdom? What solution can you create from your answer? When will you move forward and implement that solution?

What dream do you need to resurrect?

Every great dream begins with a dreamer. Always remember, you have within you the strength, the patience, and the passion to reach for the stars to change the world.

HARRIET TUBMAN

Point to Ponder:

You are the only person who can decide to pursue your dream. Books don't write themselves. Businesses don't launch themselves. You've got to take the first step and keep stepping.

What dream have you postponed? What idea has been sitting on the shelf collecting dust? What hope or vision has been left for dead in your life? Perhaps it's time to dust off that old dream and bring it back to life. So how do you do that? What's that first step that will help you get started? Coach yourself to the right answer with these powerful questions:

1. **What dream lies dormant in your life that you wish were still a possibility?**

   Sometimes we bury our dreams so deep we forget about them. Ponder for a moment. The dream it's time to dust off may be connected to your professional life, finances, relationships, health, or personal life. What is it for you right now?

2. **What do you need to give yourself permission to do about it?**

   There is a reason that something important to you has been

buried. Whatever the reason you decided you couldn't pursue it any longer, now is the time to give yourself permission. It's okay. Maybe you were hurt in the past and decided you'd be safer if you didn't go down a particular road anymore. Maybe the responsibilities of life dictated that you'd better let your dream die. Or maybe the dream seemed like it could never be achieved, so you gave up on it. Use the past as a learning tool to recast your dream. Have the faith to believe that nothing is impossible with God.

3. What do you need to say about it?

The power of life and death is in the words you speak, Proverbs 18:21 promises. Speak life into your dream right now. Say it out loud. Allow yourself to hear the words. There is power in this exercise. Speak life, not death. And watch how you talk about your dream when you discuss it with others. When you start stating all the reasons you can't have what your heart desires, you speak death to your dream. Each negative word is like a shovel, digging the grave and then piling dirt onto it until you can no longer see the dream at all. Negative words will steal your vision.

4. What action will you take next?

Faith without action is dead (James 2:17). You may have killed your dream by inaction, but you can bring it back to life by taking action, starting now. If you believe your dream is possible, you'll take steps toward it. You don't have to take all the steps at once, or even huge steps. Start with one small step, then another. Even baby steps, when taken consistently, will get you to the finish line.

My Challenge to You

Dust off that old dream! Give it new life.

Coach Yourself

Consider the dreams lying dormant in your life and respond to
the four questions above.

_____

_____

_____

_____

_____

_____

_____

_____

_____

_____

_____

_____

_____

_____

Are you ready to move into your new season?

When one door closes, another door opens; but we so often look so long and regretfully upon the closed door, that we do not see the ones which open for us.

ALEXANDER GRAHAM BELL

Point to Ponder:

Letting go of what's behind becomes easier when you create a vision for the future that excites you.

There are few things more frustrating than remaining stuck in the old when it's time to embrace something new. Sometimes the new thing is an inevitable change or transition, whether it was something you wanted or a situation that was thrust upon you. At other times, your new season is a goal you've been working toward, but you have somehow failed to notice that the thing you wished for is *here*. This new season requires you to shift your thinking so you can enjoy the vision that has finally come to fruition. Whether your new season is related to your career, relationships, finances, or health, consider these five ways to successfully step into a new phase of your life:

1. Say goodbye to the last season.

In order to fully embrace what's new, mark your passage from one season into the next. If a child is about to head off to college, plan a celebration to mark the milestone. If you are moving from one place to another, acknowledge it in a meaningful way. If you have lost someone or something important to you, grieve your loss so that you can move forward in a healthy way.

2. Embrace the new season.

Once you've said goodbye, say hello to what's new. Dive in. Consider the things you are able to do now that you couldn't before. If you're entering a difficult season, identify and embrace the help you will need to give you strength and perseverance. Acknowledge your challenges, but also be sure to open your eyes and notice the blessings too.

3. Ask, "What new habits do I need in this new season?"

What worked in the last season may not work in this new season. It's like using your old house key to try to open the door to your new home. What got you in the door there won't work here. Be flexible and adopt the new habits that will empower you to thrive in this new season.

4. Ask, "Who do I need to connect with in this new season?"

Relationships matter. Don't go it alone. Reach out and connect with those who can help you and whom you can help. When facing a major change, it's the right people who can make the difference between a smooth transition and a bumpy one.

5. Ask, "What vision am I moving toward in my new season?"

Often a new season means a new identity in some way. Perhaps your role has changed, relationships have been severed, a job was lost, or a move has put you in a totally new environment. You may have had a vision—and even achieved it—in the previous season of your life, but now it's time for something different. Your old vision may not work in this new place. What's your new vision now?

My Challenge to You

Say goodbye to an old season. Embrace your new season.

Coach Yourself

Are you ready to move into your new season? What is the evidence that you are embracing it?

Should you give up or get up?

It is not the size of the dog in the fight;
it is the size of the fight in the dog!
AFRICAN PROVERB

Point to Ponder:
When you truly commit to your goals, it becomes
easier to weather the inevitable storms.

Is there a goal you've set, but haven't really made much progress on lately? If you're like many people, the answer is yes. Whether it's a New Year's resolution you set and forgot about or a dream that just feels too hard to hold on to, it can be tempting to give up at times. Consider the goal that eludes you right now and ask yourself these five questions:

1. Do you need to break it into smaller, more bite-sized action steps?
If you force too many goals at once, you set yourself up for failure. If this is the case, all you need to do is break the goal into smaller pieces and perhaps give yourself a more palatable timeline.

2. What is the biggest obstacle to your progress?
If your goal is to eat healthier but your attempts to stay on track are sabotaged by the fact that you have to eat on the run and find yourself grabbing fast food every day for lunch, you've got a problem. Identify the obstacles that are impeding your progress.

3. What can you do to break through that obstacle?

Next, address every obstacle by brainstorming for a workable solution. That means it needs to be a solution you will actually use. Be honest with yourself about what you need. If you struggle to come up with solutions, ask someone who has already conquered the challenge you face.

4. Are you pursuing the wrong goal?

Sometimes being stuck is a way for your authentic self to put its foot down. If you can't seem to get unstuck, ask yourself, "Why is this goal so important to me? What's the purpose?" Is there another goal (perhaps even a similar goal) that resonates with you more? Choose goals aligned with your values and true priorities.

5. Are you holding on to the wrong goal just to prove you're not a quitter?

Don't fall into the trap of sticking with something that's not authentic or not working for you simply because you don't want to quit. Instead of thinking of it as quitting, think of it as making room for the right goal—the one you will be far more likely to achieve.

My Challenge to You

Before you give up, ask the right questions and answer them honestly.

Coach Yourself

Take a moment now to consider and respond to the five questions above.

What could it mean that your answer hasn't come yet?

*Life is a succession of lessons which must
be lived to be understood.*

RALPH WALDO EMERSON

Point to Ponder:

*Trusting God means getting comfortable with
not knowing all the answers.*

"I hate not knowing," a friend complained as she tried to figure out some steps to take personally and professionally. "I'm used to having a game plan, but right now I feel stuck because I honestly don't know what the right answer is. I want to plan the next stage of my life—and somehow, I feel like God's hiding the road map from me!"

If you're anything like me—or most people in the world—you like to know what's coming next in your life. But how do you handle it when you want an answer and don't get one? Maybe you've been praying for a specific answer about the next phase of your life—about a move you need to make, an important decision, a romantic partner, or another change of some sort. Yet despite the fact that you've diligently sought an answer, it simply hasn't come. It can be a frustrating place, but I invite you to make a shift and try a different approach.

I want you to consider an area of your life for which your vision looks cloudy. You don't know what you want or you just don't know what steps will be essential to take you where you want to go. Over the years I have discovered five lessons to be learned "in the meantime." The meantime is that waiting period between here and where you are destined to end up.

I've often thought I was ready for something and set out to make it happen, only later to discover that there was a great deal of growth and learning that needed to occur first. At other times it wasn't the growth and learning but some other circumstances that needed to line up in order for the vision to be fully realized. When you listen to your life, heeding the inner voice of the Holy Spirit, you set yourself up for divine timing and greater rewards than you may previously have imagined.

Ephesians 3:20 tells us that God "is able to do immeasurably more than all we ask or imagine." Waiting for your right answer is an exercise in trusting God and letting go of your attempt to control things. The truth is, we aren't in control anyway and we expend a lot of energy trying to prove to ourselves that we are.

Wherever you feel a lack of clarity, consider these five messages that may be presenting themselves to you:

1. *No* and *wait* are legitimate answers.

You regularly hear people say, "God answered my prayer," meaning they got what they asked for. But "Yes" isn't the only way God answers prayers. Sometimes He says, "No." Often He says, "Wait." All three are legitimate answers.

2. Let go of your need to know.

You can cause yourself a lot of stress by insisting that you always know what's coming. Relax and enjoy the present. Trust that all things work together for good (Romans 8:28).

3. Take a small step, then notice what happens.

If you are feeling torn about which direction to take, sometimes the best thing you can do is begin to move in one direction. Notice what happens when you do. Do you feel at peace? Are doors opening easily or is it a struggle without purpose? Sometimes taking a small step gives you clarity about whether or not to continue on a particular path.

4. Delve into an area of life you've been neglecting.

Often, we can't have what we think we are ready for because it's time to address other matters. Until those are addressed, our answer will not come. What have you been avoiding? Consider your waiting period an opportunity to face the things you've been able to avoid for a while—nurturing a relationship, taking care of yourself, going back to school, taking control of your finances, or getting your career on track. You know what it is for you. Muster up the courage to address it.

5. Connect with God by talking—and then listening.

James 4:8 says, "Come near to God and he will come near to you." As you contemplate a life change, make sure your decisions are rooted firmly in the divine guidance that is available to you when you get quiet to listen.

My Challenge to You

Stop focusing on needing to know the answers. Focus on the message that is being offered to you in the process of learning what to do next.

Coach Yourself

What answer are you waiting on? What message is being offered to you right now? What area of your life do you need to focus on while you await your answer?

Do you have the five key resilience traits?

Fall seven times. Stand up eight.

Japanese Proverb

Point to Ponder:

When thrown against the wall of adversity, you can be a tennis ball or an egg. One cracks. The other bounces back. Which will you be?

Recent years have certainly tested our collective resilience. The economic downturn and layoffs took their toll on a lot of individual lives. But even if you haven't been a victim of financial challenges, it's a safe bet you still know what it means to have a setback, whether in a relationship, your health, or dealing with any unexpected trials. What is it that allows some people to bounce back while others languish after a setback? What will empower you to become *better* as a result of a setback or challenge, rather than bitter?

Research shows that resilient people think differently. They have a set of skills—sometimes learned, other times innate—that allow them to persevere, manage stress, and triumph in the face of challenges. Here are five of the things resilient people do:

1. They are authentic.

Resilient people are at peace with their humanity. Perhaps it is because their mistakes along the way have humbled them, or life experiences have helped them accept their own vulnerability, but resilient people don't let imperfections hinder them. They don't think failing makes them a failure. They learn as they go, making course corrections that lead them to positive outcomes.

2. They are flexible thinkers.

Even if initially they struggle with negative thoughts, resilient people are self-aware enough to notice when their thinking is counterproductive. They don't fall into "thinking traps" such as jumping to conclusions or making assumptions. Instead, they gather the facts they need to move around obstacles and face the challenge head-on. If something isn't working, they make adjustments until it works. They find the aspects of the challenge that are within their control and they exercise that control. When faced with a cancer diagnosis, they change their habits to help their bodies recover. When they get passed over for promotion, they find the grain of truth in the boss's negative review and start making improvements.

3. They are (mostly) optimistic.

It's hard to bounce back from setbacks when you see every obstacle as the end of the world! Research shows that optimists live as much as nine years longer than pessimists. Seeing the bright side is good for your health and longevity. But it isn't just about simplistic positive thinking. Resilient people see risks and take precautions to prevent problems. When faced with a challenge, they are more likely to say, "I can get through this"—whether it is a tough class at school, a divorce, or a health challenge.

4. They reach out.

Resilient people don't go it alone. They have close friends and are not too proud to ask for help when they need it, talk out problems, or help others in need. When faced with a stressful situation, just knowing you have support can alleviate the pressure. Strengthen your relationships. They make you stronger.

5. They use their strengths.

Everyone has innate talents and strengths. When faced with a challenge, there is power in tapping into those strengths—the things that come naturally to you. It takes less energy to use your strengths—and in fact, you are energized by them. Know what yours are and use them.

My Challenge to You

Practice the traits of true resilience until they become second nature.

Coach Yourself

Of the five key traits of resilience shared here, which do you possess in abundance? Can you give an example of a challenging time in which you used this trait? Which of the five traits is most difficult for you? What would it take to strengthen that trait in preparation for current or future challenges?

How bright is your light?

Let your light shine before others, that they may see your good deeds and glorify your Father in heaven.

MATTHEW 5:16

Point to Ponder:

Happiness is derived from helping others, making a difference, and serving the world in your own unique way.

No matter what your purpose in life, this is an underlying mission: Living your life in such a way that people say to themselves, "There's something different about that person and I want to know how to experience some of that peace, joy, and love in my own life."

Matthew 5:14-16 says, "You are the light of the world. A town built on a hill cannot be hidden. Neither do people light a lamp and put it under a bowl. Instead they put it on its stand, and it gives light to everyone in the house. In the same way, let your light shine before others, that they may see your good deeds and glorify your Father in heaven." Here are five ways you can exemplify this principle:

1. Look for ways to be a blessing.

Letting your light shine means letting all that is good within you come forth. There is so much negativity swirling around us on a daily basis that when good enters our environment, it brings light to the darkness. It is a refreshing burst of clean air. Be sensitive to the needs of others. Find ways to be a blessing— even simple ways such as being a courteous driver, thoughtful friend, and kind coworker.

2. Refuse to be judgmental.

One of the fastest ways to turn people away from God is to judge them. You can acknowledge that a person has done wrong without condemning them for it. Remember that all have sinned and fall short of the glory of God. We've all done things for which we needed to be forgiven, and by grace, we have received forgiveness. Be merciful to others. Choose to pray for those you feel tempted to judge. Embrace and support them when they are trying to do better. When you do this, they will be more likely to be curious about the faith you profess.

3. Speak up for what is just.

Speak up for what is just—not *right*. Too often, we confuse *being* right with *doing* right. Focus more on the latter. In every instance and every conflict, it is essential that you treat people justly. Ensure that those who cross your path are better off for having done so. If you are in a work or personal situation in which others are being cheated, disrespected, or done a disservice, let your light shine and speak up. You can do so in a way that is direct, calm, straightforward, and nonjudgmental.

4. Let go of the desire to fit in.

It's not easy to let your light shine if you feel a need to fit in everywhere you go. In some environments, simply smiling and speaking to people in a kind way will cause you to seem odd. Choose to be more concerned with being a vessel of truth and love on a daily basis than fitting in with the world's standards.

5. Don't hide your spiritual life.

One of the most common ways you can dim your own light is to pretend publicly that God is not central to your way of life. If God is an important part of who you are, why would you make your relationship private and keep it to yourself?

Why would you present a public face that never acknowledges your own spirituality? You don't need a Bible on your desk or a preacher's robe to share your faith with others. When opportunities present themselves to share where your strength comes from in difficult times, or to acknowledge how God has protected or blessed you, be honest. Your faith is a part of who you are. When you free yourself to be who you are, you also free others to be who they truly are.

My Challenge to You

Identify at least one way you will share your light this week. Then intentionally set out to be a vessel of love and light in the world.

Coach Yourself

In what ways have you dimmed your light? How can you go about becoming a brighter light that attracts others to God by the way you live your life and treat others?

Will you let go of the old to make room for the new?

Some people believe holding on and hanging in there are signs of great strength. However, there are times when it takes much more strength to know when to let go and then do it.

ANN LANDERS

Point to Ponder:

The ability to let go of the old and embrace the new is an important resilience skill.

When I bought my first condo back in the 90s, I decided to replace the handles on every cabinet and drawer in the kitchen and the bathrooms. I went to a design center and picked out new handles, unscrewed all the old ones, and replaced them with the shiny, new modern ones. Then I did a peculiar thing. I put the 25 or 30 old handles in individual plastic baggies and stored them "just in case" I might need them again later. It was silly, really. I couldn't stand those handles. They were ugly. They were outdated. There was no way I would use them again! And yet I couldn't bring myself to throw them out. Maybe someone else might want them, I told myself. I doubted it, but just in case, I kept them and they helped clutter up my storage space.

Why is it so hard to let go? Whether it's old e-mail or a worn-out sweater, outdated files or a toxic friendship, sometimes we hold on to things for too long. They serve no purpose but to clutter our lives unnecessarily. Today, I want to challenge you to face your fear of letting go.

There are a few common fears that appear when it's time to let go of something. What are you hanging on to even though it's time to let go? Which of these pesky fears is it time to face?

- **fear that you won't have what you need in the future**

- **fear of being wrong**

- **fear of loneliness**

- **fear of regret**

Breaking through fear requires one key factor: courage. Courage requires faith and trust that your future will be okay without the thing you are letting go of. And you can muster up the courage to let go by coaching yourself with questions that will help you get unstuck, such as:

- **What does my intuition tell me about letting go in this situation? Will I follow it?**

- **If the thing I fear most happens, what is my plan B?**

- **Who could I ask to hold me accountable and encourage me as I let go?**

Make a decision. Carve out some time to do what you need to do. You can do it. By the way, I let go of my old cabinet handles. And I've never once needed them or missed them. Imagine that!

My Challenge to You

There is something it's time to let go of. You know what it is. Muster up the courage and just do it. You'll feel lighter for it.

Coach Yourself

Answer these questions:

- What does your intuition tell you about letting go in this situation?

- What if you let go? What will happen then? And then what will you do?

- If the thing you fear most happens, what is your plan B?

- Who could you ask to hold you accountable and encourage you as you let go?

Can you just wait till morning?

Weeping may stay for the night, but rejoicing comes in the morning.

PSALM 30:5

Point to Ponder:

When you are led by fear rather than faith, you can usurp the blessings that are headed your way.

On a business trip to Colorado Springs years ago, some unconventional accommodations got the best of my imagination and taught me a lesson I'll never forget. I had received a generous invitation from a staff member at Glen Eyrie Castle and Conference Center to stay at no expense in the biggest and nicest room at their retreat center. The property, a castle built by a Civil War general for his wife, was established in the late 19th century and was nestled in the foothills near picturesque Pike's Peak.

I'd been told the location was beautiful, but it was dark when a colleague and his wife brought me to the location. Upon proceeding through the gate, I began to feel a bit apprehensive. We drove along a winding road with no streetlights and small, dark cottages sprinkled here and there. It seemed like the scene just before something crazy happens in a scary movie. Just after 10:00 p.m. we pulled up to the home I'd be staying in. One light was on in the house and I thought I saw a man sitting at a desk near a front window. We walked up to the large, ornate wooden door with a heavy metal knocker. Taped to the center of the door was a note with *Valorie* scribbled on the outside and a key inside. It instructed me to the location of my room inside this bed-and-breakfast-style cottage.

We walked through the foyer, then a long, stately dining room with a fireplace and seating for 14 people, and finally a vast living area with paintings of people I imagined were long gone. The lighting was nearly nonexistent, and as we proceeded through the house I thought, *Where am I? Who else is in this house? Are the former inhabitants still with us?* I knew I was being silly, but the thoughts and questions were gaining speed. We arrived at my room—a spacious pink bedroom with a long hall entryway, an antique canopy bed, living area, work area, and a huge bathroom. My friend saw the apprehension on my face. And his wife looked a little apprehensive about leaving me there too.

"You don't have to stay here," he assured me. "We can go to the Hilton right now if you want." I gazed through one of the dozen ten-foot-high windows in the room. It was pitch black outside and I couldn't see a thing. I wasn't feeling excited about staying. But, as I told my friend, it was such a generous offer, and I would feel terrible about leaving to check into a hotel.

Just then, I heard a motherly voice call out my name. I turned to find a lovely older couple—the home's hosts—enter the room.

The husband, perhaps sensing a little tension by the way we were scoping out the room, said lightly, "Don't worry. There are no ghosts here. It just looks like this because you came at night."

A little embarrassed, I said, "Oh, I'm sure it's lovely in the daytime," hoping I was right.

The host's wife proceeded to tell me a few things about the room and the house. She said something about an unconventional wake-up call at 5:30 a.m., but I thought she was kidding. They wished me a good night before retiring to their room.

"Well," I said to my friend and his wife, "I'll stay tonight and let's see how it goes."

"I'll be back to pick you up in the morning," he offered. "Just pack your bags if you want to check into a hotel tomorrow, and we'll take them when I pick you up."

Uneasy, but undeterred, I readied for bed and decided that my apprehension was unfounded (but left the hallway light on for good measure.

Around 5:20 the next morning, I was suddenly awakened by the sound of a woman laughing—well, kind of cackling. It was almost a giggle—little short, choppy bursts of laughter. The first time I heard it, I thought it was a bit strange. The second time, I thought, "Boy, something must really be funny." I tried to go back to sleep, but she wouldn't stop her funny little giggles.

"What could be that funny this early in the morning?" I thought, now feeling a bit annoyed.

Then it occurred to me! The hostess had warned me the night before that I would get a wake-up call around 5:30 in the morning from wild turkeys gobbling outside. I jumped out of bed and looked outside, only to see huge wild black turkeys shuffling about on the lawn. In the background was a spectacular mountain view, and I could see the edges of a large stone castle peeking from behind the tall evergreen trees on the property. The scene from the 12 expansive windows in my room was captivating. I took a deep breath of gratitude and inhaled the divine beauty of nature. Then I laughed at myself for my reaction the night before. During my three days at Glen Eyrie, I took walks, meditated, and enjoyed the scenic landscape and peaceful environment that surrounded me.

I gleaned a simple lesson from this story: Sometimes you have to persevere through the uncertainty of darkness to experience the beautiful vision that comes when light is shed on a situation. Things aren't always as they seem, especially when we have a limited view.

In what area of your life are you apprehensive because you can't see what's coming? Are you ready to bail out quickly before you can see the whole picture? I offer you a challenge: Refuse to allow irrational fears to pressure you into making hasty decisions—whether in your personal or professional life. "Weeping may stay for the night, but rejoicing comes in the morning," Psalm 30:5 promises. Stick around and see what God has in store before you take it upon yourself to "fix things."

When you finally see what morning looks like, you may just find you were in the right place all along.

My Challenge to You

Be patient. Refuse to make a hasty decision. Instead, endure a little discomfort until you can see the bigger picture and can make a more informed decision.

Coach Yourself

In what area of your life are you tempted to make a premature decision? Is God prompting you to wait a little while longer before showing you the bigger picture?

This isn't the way you planned it, is it?

*What the caterpillar calls the end of the world
the master calls a butterfly.*

RICHARD BACH

Point to Ponder:

Adaptability is a hallmark of resilience.

Do you ever feel like life just isn't going the way you planned it? Perhaps you find yourself on the verge of giving up on a dream. Your job search seems fruitless. A relationship keeps hitting a brick wall. You get a little extra money, and then an unexpected expense saps the money as quickly as you got it. Sometimes life is about plowing ahead when the road gets long and hard. When you feel exhausted and weary, that's when it is essential that you take charge before you burn out or give up.

Like you, I've been there. One of the best skills you can gain in life is the ability to navigate the unexpected turns and setbacks life throws your way. Life doesn't always go the way we plan it. In fact, it rarely does. Let your challenges build the kind of character and perseverance that will empower you to stay the course and win the race that's been set out for you. Here's how:

1. Stop expecting things to be easy.

One of the quickest ways to become discouraged is to expect life to unfold just the way you planned it, with few or no obstacles or opposition. When you expect challenges, you're not surprised when they appear. Don't get caught in the trap of feeling sorry for yourself when hard times come. Instead, use it as an opportunity to tap into your strengths, character, and faith to courageously face whatever life throws your way.

2. Get some fresh air.

When your thoughts begin a downward spiral, it often means you need a break. Have you been ruminating about your problems, rehashing them over and over in your mind? Take a walk. Do something different. Get out of your normal environment. It can energize you and redirect your thoughts.

3. Get some perspective.

While fresh air will give you perspective, so will someone else's life. When you start focusing too much on what's wrong in your life, force yourself to notice what's right. Right now, stop and acknowledge three things you are grateful for. You probably can't stop at three! Then open your eyes to others' stories of resilience. You are not the first person to face your challenges. Who else has gone through them with strength and grace? Realizing you are not alone is powerful. In the process, you may also discover someone who has triumphed through far more difficult challenges and can serve as a source of inspiration.

4. Commit to running your race to the best of your ability.

Who knows why you are going through what you are going through? It may not even be worth the energy of attempting to figure it out. What is worth your energy is expanding your character and capacity in the process. In what ways will you become a better person by persevering through this? What growth do you intend to glean through it all?

5. Be an inspiration.

For my book *Where Will You Go From Here?* I interviewed

people who had navigated major life crises—from job loss to divorce to cancer to the loss of a child. My intention was to provide inspiration and examples for my readers as I dutifully set out to conduct interviews with each person. But I found the interviews were as much for me as for the reader. Each person inspired me profoundly through their attitude, determination, and faith. Tackle your challenges in such a way that your children, friends, family, and coworkers will be inspired by your example. You can give others hope by simply acting with the courage to live and love fully in the face of fear and disappointment.

My Challenge to You

Make a decision to allow your setbacks to build character and perseverance. You can recover from your setback a better person.

Coach Yourself

What do you need to accept? In what ways is it time to stop feeling sorry for yourself? Where can you find some perspective that will inspire and empower you to persevere despite your setback? When you get discouraged, what thought will lift you up?

What could you do to feel happier right now?

Most people are about as happy as they make up their minds to be.

ABRAHAM LINCOLN

Point to Ponder:

Happiness is the one thing we pursue for its own sake. Most other things in life—whether relationships, health, money, career options—we pursue because we believe they will make us happy.

Is it one of those days? Someone's not pulling their weight at work, leaving you with a heavier workload. Or you ran late again, and started the day off on the wrong foot. Your spouse said something that rubbed you the wrong way or you got some bad news. Or maybe nothing particularly bad happened—you just don't feel all that happy. Whatever the case, improving your mood is something within your control.

These three simple mood-boosters won't change your coworker, your spouse, or the fact that life simply isn't going your way right now, but they will make you feel better while you're dealing with the stress:

1. **Write your three best things.**

   Identify the three best things that happened to you in the last 48 hours. It can be something really simple, like the fact that you found a parking space close to the door at the post office or the kiss your child gave you before going to school this morning. Gratitude immediately shifts your focus back to the good things in your life. Even when things are going badly, there is something you can find to be grateful for.

2. Reach out to someone who makes you laugh, smile, and feel great.

"A cheerful heart is good medicine," says Proverbs 17:22. And it's true. Being around positive people, especially those who know how to laugh and have fun, can be an instant pick-me-up. Who is that person for you? Stop by their desk. Call them up. Make dinner plans. Be intentional about spending time with people who make you smile and limit your time with those who do the opposite.

3. Know what brings you joy and do it.

What brings you joy? Whatever it is, find a way to incorporate it into your day today. In the midst of a hectic schedule and back-to-back activities it can be easy to squeeze out those simple pleasures, but don't. Make them non-negotiable, especially today.

My Challenge to You

Take control of your happiness by doing something that will intentionally boost your mood.

Coach Yourself

What are your three biggest blessings of the day? Who brings you joy? What brings you joy?

Coaching Toolkit

When you ask the right questions, you get the right answers. Use these questions to coach yourself and get inspired. You may want to journal about them or work with a friend or coach to explore your answers.

- How would you describe your best possible future self?

- What's your most meaningful short-term goal? What's your most meaningful long-term goal?

- What's the most pressing problem you need to solve in your life right now?

- What issue, if unresolved, threatens to sabotage your dream?

- What is it time for you to learn?

- What is your personal mission statement?

- What desire of your heart are you most afraid to hope for out of fear you will not get it?

- What would it take to find the courage to fight for that desire despite your fear?

- Ten years from now, what will you wish you had done?

- If you could not fail, what would you attempt?

- What lesson have you learned from your biggest failure or mistake?

- In what way do you need to apply that lesson to a current opportunity or challenge?

- Where do you see yourself one year from now?

- How would you describe a scene from a typical day in your life a decade from now?

- What legacy do you want to create for the children in your life?

- In what way are you settling because you've given up the belief that something better is possible?

- Who inspires you and why?

- What have you always wanted to do, but haven't yet? What date will you set for that goal?

- What do you do that seems to cause time to fly by? How often could you engage in that activity?

- What is it time to let go of in order to make room for something new to come into your life?

- What are you looking forward to this week? If nothing, what fun activity could you schedule?

- How would you describe the season of life you are in right now? What is the next season?

- What energizes you?

- Think back to a time when you were at your best. What inspired you?

- If you had a life list of things you want to do before your life is over what would be in your top 50?

Conclusion

Seven Sacred Ways to Live Your Best Life

Since you picked up this book, I imagine you, like me, love reading and learning new strategies for how to live your best life. But the best advice I've ever found has come from the words of Jesus. My message here is simple. In fact, it isn't my message at all. I'd like to share seven messages that Jesus taught during His three years of public ministry.

Do not worry about tomorrow, for tomorrow will worry about itself (Matthew 6:34). Too often in life, we worry about issues that work themselves out over time. Worrying does not change anything. It is a waste of time, energy, and life itself. Plan your steps, but refuse to allow fear of what might go wrong to consume you. Instead, focus on what you can do in the present moment to create the kind of future you want.

Do not judge, and you will not be judged (Luke 6:37). There may be people in your life right now who are doing things you don't agree with, perhaps even engaging in behavior that is destructive to them. Choose to love them and pray for them without judgment. Choose compassion and empathy, perhaps even tough love, but reserve judgment.

Be careful not to practice your righteousness in front of others to be seen by them (Matthew 6:1). Do good and treat people well because it is the right thing to do, not because of the accolades or rewards you might receive from others. Make sure your motives are pure.

For those who exalt themselves will be humbled, and those who humble themselves will be exalted (Matthew 23:12). Humility is freedom—freedom from the pressure to be perfect, keep up appearances, or be better than everyone else. Success is a combination of working hard and being blessed with opportunities, abilities, and people who support you. None of us achieves or succeeds solely by our own power. Don't worry about taking credit or making yourself look good. Focus on serving, learning, and loving, and the rewards will come.

Everything is possible for one who believes (Mark 9:23). Consider your biggest dream for your life. It is not enough to say you will achieve it. You must believe it. You may not know exactly how it will become true for you. Your first step is to simply believe it's possible. Say it out loud and often: *It's possible!* With God, all things are possible.

For God so loved the world that he gave his one and only Son, that whoever believes in him shall not perish but have eternal life (John 3:16). Most people know this Scripture as a foundational statement for the Christian faith. But there is something I find intriguing in its wording. It is the connection between loving and giving. God loved us, and therefore He gave. When you love others you give of yourself, sometimes in very unselfish and sacrificial ways. Saying you love someone is not enough. Give of yourself—your time, energy, affection, and resources, and they will truly know you love them.

Then you will know the truth, and the truth will set you free (John 8:32). The truth sets you free in many ways. Be truthful with yourself about the issues of your life. Speak truth into your relationships. Countless relationships fail because one person or both are unwilling to speak from their hearts. Be truthful about what you want and what you are afraid of, and you will gain the strength to step fully into the rich, abundant life you were created to live.

My Challenge to You

Spend time reading the Word and glean ancient wisdom that is as relevant today as it was in the beginning.

Coach Yourself

Which of these seven Scriptures most resonates with where you are in your life right now? Why? What message do you sense that Scripture is speaking to your situation?

It has been an honor to walk with you through these pages. I hope you will revisit them often as you look for the answers you need and the right questions to help you discover them!

Warmest wishes,

Valorie Burton

Valorie Burton is a certified personal and executive coach who has served hundreds of clients in over 40 states and eight countries. She is founder and director of The Coaching and Positive Psychology Institute and the author of eight books on personal development. She is deeply committed to helping people be more resilient so they can thrive in life and work, be more productive, and live with balance and purpose.

Join more than 25,000 subscribers to her weekly e-newsletter, *The Coaching Session*, at
www.valorieburton.com

To learn more about books by Valorie Burton or to read sample chapters, log on to our website:
www.harvesthousepublishers.com

Successful Women Think Differently

9 Habits to Make You Happier, Healthier, and More Resilient

Popular author and professional certified coach Valorie Burton knows that successful women think differently. They make decisions differently. They set goals differently and bounce back from failure differently. Valorie is dedicated to helping women create new thought processes that empower them to succeed in their relationships, finances, work, health, and spiritual life. With new, godly habits, women will discover how to:

- focus on solutions, not problems
- choose courage over fear
- nurture intentional relationships
- take consistent action in the direction of their dreams
- build the muscle of self-control

In this powerful and practical guide, Valorie provides a woman with insight into who she really is and gives her the tools, knowledge, and understanding to succeed.